The LOWDOWN On WITCHES

Also by Leonard Low:

Scotland's Untold Stories
Largo's Untold Stories
St Andrews' Untold Stories

The Weem Witch
The Battle of St Monans

The LOWDOWN On WITCHES

TRUE STORIES OF SCOTTISH WITCH TRIALS

LEONARD LOW

AUTHOR OF *THE WEEM WITCH* AND
SCOTLAND'S UNTOLD STORIES

GUARDBRIDGE BOOKS
ST ANDREWS, SCOTLAND

Published by Guardbridge Books,
St Andrews, Fife, United Kingdom.

http://guardbridgebooks.co.uk

Lowdown on Witches, The

Copyright © 2022 by Leonard Low. All rights reserved.

Apart from any fair use for the purposes of research, private study, criticism or review, as permitted under the Copyrights, Design and Patents Act 1988, this publication may not be reproduced in any written, electronic, recording, or photocopying manner without written permission of the publisher or author. Enquires concerning reproduction terms should be sent to the publisher.

Cover Photograph: © Eduard Goricev | Dreamstime.com

ISBN: 978-1-911486-73-2

The following 30 chapters are from the dates 966–1727 in Scotland. I catalogue the events of these trials alphabetically from the parish that was pursuing the Witch hunt or the title of the piece of interest.

The odd one out is the trial of Jean Maxwell (chapter 16), a case that was outwith the years of terminating Witches in 1805. Although the death penalty was abolished, the crime still carried a prison sentence. But how lucky she was; 70 years earlier and she most definitely would have burnt!

CHAPTERS

Acknowledgements xi
Foreword xiii
BRANDING xix
THE MONSTRUOUS REGIMENT OF WOMEN xxv
1. ANSTRUTHER Wester Parish, 1643. 1
2. AYRSHIRE, 1576 9
3. BRECHIN Parish Burnings 15
4. BUTE, 1632–1673 21
5. CAIRNEY Parish 27
6. CRAIL Parish, 1599–1643 33
7. CROOK OF DEVON Parish, 1662. 39
8. CULROSS, Parish, 1621–1684 45
9. DORNOCH, The Devil's Horseshoe, 1727 55
10. DUNBAR, Isobel Young, 1629 65

11. DUNDEE, Grissel Jaffrey, 1669 71
12. DUNDEE, The Naked Schneckle Eaters, 1641...... 81
13. EDINBURGH, Madness of Major Weir, 1670 87
14. FORFAR, 1661 95
15. FORRES, The Real Macbeth Witches, 966 103
16. IRVINE, 1618–1650 111
17. KIRKCUDBRIGHT, Jean Maxwell, 1805......... 119
18. KIRKLISTON, Heart Attack, 1655 125
19. LARGO, 1697–60 131
20. MUNLOCHY, The Suddie Witches, 1699........ 147
21. PAISLEY, The Bargarren Witches, 1697 153
22. PITTENWEEM, The Weem Witch, 1597–1705 .. 163
23. PRESTONPANS, Isobel Grierson, 1607 171
24. PERTH, The Mysterious Maggie Wall 177
25. POLLOCKSHAW, The Bewitching of Sir George Maxwell, 1677 183
26. ST ANDREWS, 1588......................... 189
27. ST MONANS, Maggie Morgan, 1651............ 195
28. STRATHGLASS WITCHES, 1662............... 201
29. TORRYBURN, 1705 207
30. THURSO, The TRANSMOGGYFIER, 1718...... 217
NAMES OF FIFE ACCUSED WITCHES 223
AFTERWORD.................................... 229

Location of the Stories by Chapter

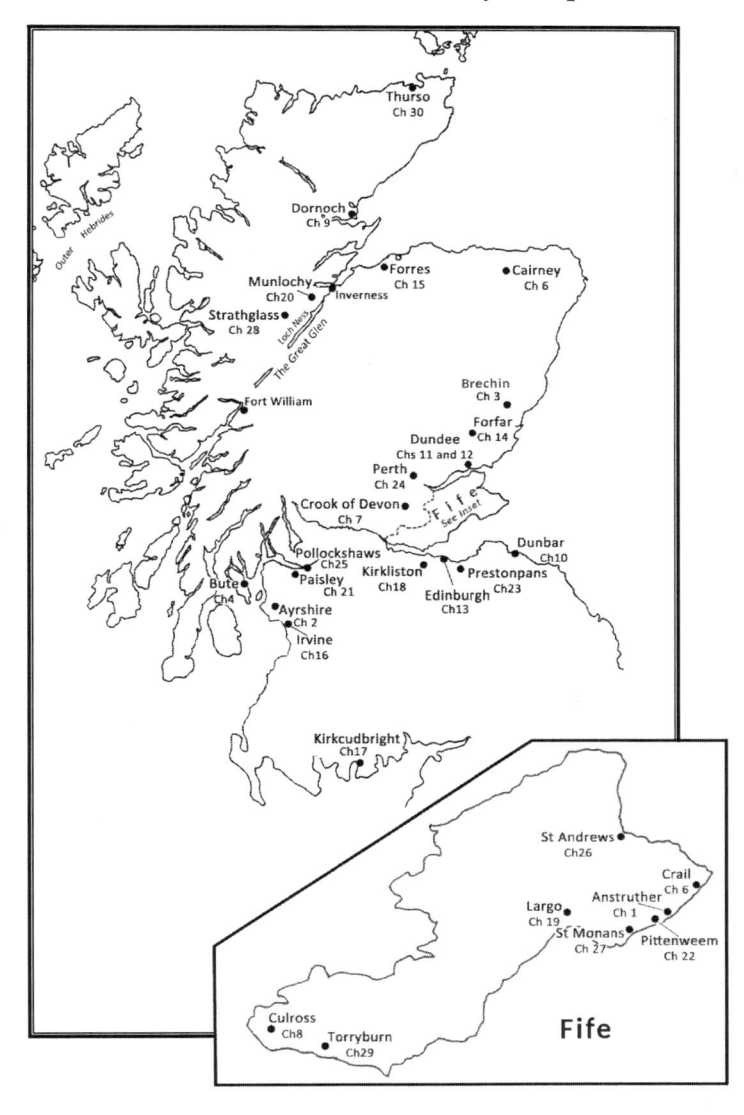

Leonard Low was born in Upper Largo, a small village in Fife. He has a residency in *Haunted Magazine*, is a consistent contributor to *The Courier* newspaper, been filmed for BBC Alba, acted as a consultant to the *Outlander* TV series, and he is a lecturer and speaker on the subjects of his many books and Scottish Witch trials. He's the Author of *The Weem Witch, Largo's Untold Stories, St Andrews' Untold Stories, The Battle of St Monans,* and *Scotland's Untold Stories*. Leonard lives with Ruth in Leven, Fife, and has two daughters, Amber and Kirsty, and a son, Callum, a cat called Floki, a dog called Louie, and several hens.

Acknowledgements

I'm writing this the day I get my first Covid 19 jab. Any following mutations that affect me will be blamed for any following mistakes in this book's text. What a mad year 2020/21 was. I had my last book *Scotland's Untold Stories* launch, then stall as distribution was destroyed by illness due to Covid. Then the book, finally, after a month's limbo, reached the shops, only for them to then close for the next 5 months. I had three lucrative lectures at the 600 seat Glenrothes Halls cancelled because of Covid, and the financial repercussions of this were huge! My first online kindle exploration helped keep the book in the public eye, as did my appearance on TV in *Men In Kilts* with the very nice Hollywood actors Sam Heughan and Graham MacTavish. The death toll to this modern plague of Covid 19, which if it had happened 300 years earlier, would most definitely have had hundreds of Witches questioned and blamed for it to add to the tales in this book.

Several magazines once again helped push my books; hats off to *St Andrews in Focus*, *Fortean Times*, and *Haunted Magazine*, all at BBC Alba for filming in Pittenweem with me, and of course all at Starz for *Men in Kilts* ep 4—see you again soon for next season—and BBC radio York and BBC Scotland for interviews. With lockdown came dozens of Zoom meetings, and I was happy to be the foil for those that asked me. Thanks to Glenrothes Halls, Jim Parker and his group, Naomi at Falkirk library, Ewan Irvine at the Sir Arthur Conan Doyle Centre, and the many others who have helped. That my colleague in ghostly investigations and documentaries, sound engineer Rodger Wilson, gets top billing in my credits is no more than his due. He motivates, doesn't freak out when on a haunting as a poltergeist smashes plates around us, loves a good gig or two, and never laughed too much when an electric fence did me in the goolies when we were making our documentary on *The Weem Witch*... thanks pal!

My love as always to these following very lovely Witches' peculiars who do their master's bidding... Bruce and Kay Marshall, William Mclean, Steven 'Sherpa boy' Gilfeather, John Van Dieken (first man to cycle down Largo Law—also first in casualty!), David Baxter, Hugh Mackay and Anya, Irish Jocky (by the way), Billy Morris and Ian Muirhead, Jamie (up the Rams), Paula Wilson, Linda and Bill Whitford, Mr and Mrs David Low, Kirsten, and my little big ones: Callum Low, Kirsty Low, and Amber St Clair-Case.

I must thank all at Creative Scotland; without their generous Author Fund grants, I would have struggled to construct this volume, and Guardbridge Books who inherited a rocky road with our Covid 19 problems, but thanks David for having faith.

And last of all... she actually turned down dinner with Hollywood James Bond potential and *Outlander* boys Sam Heughan and Graham McTavish when we were filming *Men In Kilts* as she would rather go home and watch telly!!!... to the frustrations of millions of red-blooded women!... but when she's got me, she doesn't need venison when there's mince at home! Love you Ruth... X

Heretic in the Bible teachings had to be burned! The Bible states:

> If a man abide not in me, he is cast forth as a branch and is withered and men gathered. Then cast them into the fire and they are burned!
> —John XV:6

This behaviour stalled the advances of medicines for 300 years by killing the curious and those brave pioneers who through trial and error had found the right herbs and minerals to cure illnesses and heal.

Those who were themselves experimental in herbs and medicines were now looked on with suspicion as conjurers of magic and servants of Satan. Completely unfairly treated after their hard efforts in administrating cures had been successful, but in the eyes of the Church, as when the work of prayers had failed and a simple peasant woman's herbs had worked, the chant of "Witch" was never far away (look to our St Andrews chapter and see the thanks the Archbishop of St Andrews gave his healers!).

I always wondered, while being brought up in Upper Largo, to look up high level to the parish church walls where it states in a stone carving… "FEAR GOD". From the Witch burning years, we had every reason from the figures known to be scared witless!

This is a book long in the making. Each case and chapter here have been meticulously examined from primary sources—books I have obtained and added to my library at immense costs over the years to form an impressive but sad obituary to the thousands of Witches found... some of my first editions on Witch trials and original manuscripts are from 1637. I own manuscripts directly involved in the Bargarran hunts of 1697 and some concerning Sir George Maxwell, a court judge who condemned many a Witch and was supposedly bewitched to death himself, five burned because of it (both have their stories in here).

I own a pair of scissors used on the Pittenweem Witches and have the very Witch Pricker that bled them! I own two Bellarmine Witch bottles, one with 1600 stamped as its manufacture date that was found in the walls of a house in Charles Street, Pittenweem. I also have a lead seal from the Witch hating Pope Innocent VIII who gave Papal authority to the *Malleus Maleficarum* book.

As I was born and live on the Fife coast, the numbers taken and processed through the courts fascinate and sicken in equal measures.

But where are my manners? First meetings deserve introductions. My name is Leonard Low. This book you are holding is a product of the Witch hunts in Scotland. From documenting ancient source records, more than half these following chapters are in print for the first time the tales—taken from diaries and parish records never explored by other authors before this volume. Each one is very different, and some are actually hilarious in the Church's attempts to find the accused guilty. These cases are from the Scottish shores, and I have carefully visited each area to map out what the tourist can see today of the history of the trial.

From a Largo Fifer who was never baptised and has three nipples (you better believe it!), my time living in the Witch hunting years of 1563–1736 would have been very limited. Indeed, my ancestor met the flames in 1644 St Andrews.

Naturally, my heart lies in the coastal Fife cases, and with this I must dedicate this latest book from me to the east coast Witches… from Kirkcaldy to Crail… the ones identified and known by name are mentioned at the end of the book.

EDITOR'S NOTE: Names were not written consistently in the 17th century. Some people's names may be spelled differently in different documents, or even within the same document! Therefore, giving a definitive spelling of a name from time is impossible. Where possible, we tried to use the spelling from the oldest document, or trial records. These may not be consistent with other accounts. At times this even introduces confusion over whether two differently spelled names refer to the same person. One does one's best. Such is the nature of working with historic documents.

BRANDING

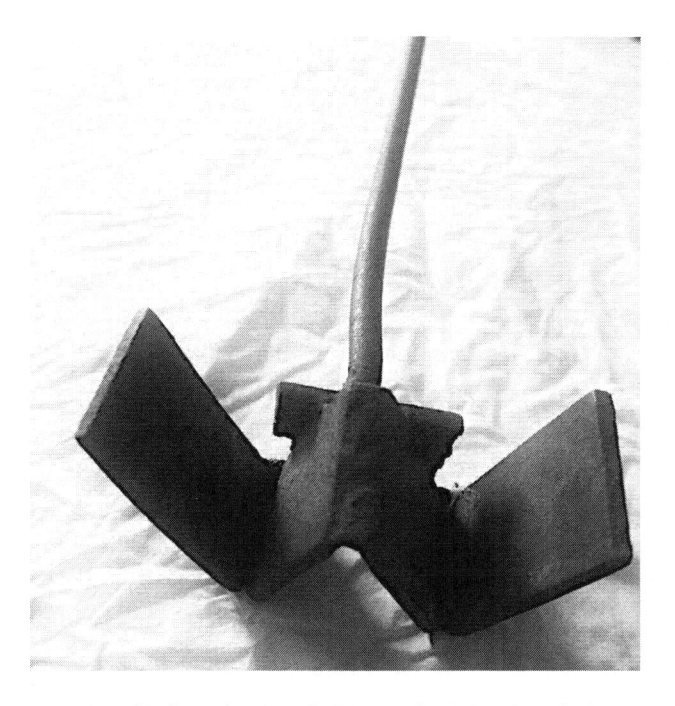

Scotland's first king of the unified lands of the Gaels and Picts was Kenneth MacAlpin. Around the year 697, he set down laws based on biblical teachings, ordaining that "jugglers, Wizards, Necromancers and such that do call up spirits and use to seek upon them for help, let them be burnt to death."

This is our earliest such mention of Witchcraft in Scotland. Again, in the time of King Duff, 962–966, manuscripts mention him troubled by some Witches in the village of Forres near Inverness. The Witches are accused of making a waxen image of him and sticking pins in it. The

Witches are dealt with in horrific fashion. Three women are rammed alive into wooden barrels at the top of a hill and secured inside. Then huge nails are driven into the sides, and the barrels are turned on their sides and set off bouncing down the hill... where they stopped, the barrels were set alight and the resulting mince inside was burnt to ashes.

In 1537, Lady Glamis, Lady Jane Douglas, sister to the Earl of Angus, was burnt on the Castlehill of Edinburgh. Her charge was plotting the death of King James V with Witchcraft... but her death was more inspired by politics than the *Maleficarum*. But the charge served its purpose.

Before the 1563 Witchcraft Act, parishes had no real zest for hunting Witches. But, when need be, they were found, arrested, and either humiliated in public churches or banished from a town's borders. To be banished doesn't sound too harsh, but it left you to the mercy of thieves and robbers in the "no man's land" between parishes. To mark you as banished, the parish that was expelling you would take an iron brand, heat it in a fire, and burn a mark identifying you for your crime, usually on the cheek. The above photo of a Brander would burn a clear "V" and "M" when pushed harder, giving you the "VM" brand representing "Virgin Mary" to cleanse you of your crime.

It wasn't till the Witchcraft Act in Queen Mary's 9th Parliament of 1563 that courts and parishes took the threat of Witchcraft seriously and with any rigour and enthusiasm. The penalty system made any Witch found and incarcerated in village jails very expensive and problematic to find a willing relative to cover the expenses. In the Act, following the recommendations of the *Malleus Maleficarum* as its blueprint, all goods and land belonging to a Witch would be seized by the civil authorities (Church and Councils) when a guilty verdict was revealed. All well and good if the Witches found had property, but the mitigation process and wheels of procedure in terminating a Witch in the fires of a burning stake were massively expensive.

The burning of Alison Dick and William Coke in Kirkcaldy, in 1633, brought a bill for £34, 11 shillings. That's ropes, wood, tar barrels, jail, and torture fees. That in today's money would be... £318.61, which doesn't look very expensive but was enough for 37 days wages in the 1600s, according to The National Archives Currency converter. The Scottish pound was worth 13 to the English pound at this time.

Aberdeen in 1597 started a terrible Witch hunt involving around eighty people in which at least forty went to the flames. The town's bill for the Witches incarcerated from 1596 May–1597 March still exist: thirteen months imprisonment involving forty-four Witches; of whom two committed suicide in prison, two were found not guilty, six were banished, and the other thirty-four were strangled and burnt at the stake. The hefty load from its thirteen-month jail term to execution cost £177 pounds, 17 shillings and 4 pence Scots money. That's 273 days for a tradesman's wage in 1597.

> Item, the 23d day of May, 1597, gevin to Gilbert Bairnis, be vertew of ane ordinance of counsall for sustentatioun of the witches in prisin fra the 16th of Marche, 1596, to the 23d of May nixt, thairefter debursit be him upon their ordinar chargis, — £50 13 4
> Item, to Alex. Reid, smythe, for twa pair of scheckills to the witches in the stepill, — 1 12 0
> Item, to Thomas Dicksoun, in recompence of his halbert broken at the execusion of the witches, 1 10 0
> Item, to Johne Justice, for burning upon the cheik of four several persones suspect of witchcraft, and banischet, — 1 6 8
> Item, gevin to Alex. Home, for mackin off joggis, stepills, and lockis to the witches during the haill tyme foirsaid, — 2 6 8
> Christian Mitchell, Bessie Thom, Isobell Barroun. Item, the 9th of March, 1596, for ane boll and a half of collis to burn the said witches, — 1 10 0
> Item, for threttie-five loads of peattis, — 3 10 0
> Item, for six tar barrellis, — 2 0 0
> Item, for tua irne barrellis, — 0 8 0
> Item, for a staik, dressing and setting of it, — 0 16 8
>
> Carry forward, — £65 13 4

We can see from the itemised bill above—A bill from Aberdeen showing the Branding bill—it was for four Witches, being John Leyis (Lewis?) and his daughters Elspeth, Jonat, and Violat, who have all been banished and branded. The bill for that being £1, 6 shilling and 8 pence Scots, or in 1600, two day's wages.

A painful result and cast out into the wilderness, but the burnings continued for another year at least in Aberdeen.

The Pittenweem Witch hunt of 1704/5, which I covered in my book *The Weem Witch*, lasted barely a year. It involved the arrest of nine people (one, a man, was released early). The others went through a nightmare orchestrated by an insane and determined minister. One (an old man) was tortured to death in his tolbooth cell, another was murdered and mutilated by an angry mob. As the parish hadn't secured a proper commission before proceeding with the tortures on the Witches, the weight of the government lawyers fell on the parish, exposing a young boy who the minister had used as his puppet to get his desired hatred of Witches across the Presbytery.[1] This episode in horror in 1704/5 cost Pittenweem a whopping £194, 11 shillings for the expenses. That figure was £13, 14 shillings and 4 pence over the annual expenditure for the entire parish.

To Pittenweem's shame, on the order to release the Witches from Parliament, the parish was so angry they couldn't prosecute the Witches, they would only release them if the Witch accused paid up front £8 as a bond for her own release. The fees were found and paid by these poverty-stricken, tortured souls, some selling their last item of value; their grave shroud, that being a white sheet intended to wrap them up decently when they died. It was law in 1686 when King James VII passed an Act of Parliament to aid the linen industry, "that no person whatsoever of high or low degree should be buried in any shirt, sheet or anything else except in plain linen or cloth spun within the kingdom." It came with a penalty of £300 Scots pounds.

Although the Ministry could gain massive collective power over its congregation in fear of Witches and the belief that the Church could protect them, it could take a few wealthy Witches' deaths to actually balance the books; all property and wealth finding its way into the Church's hands if proven guilty of Witchcraft.

---

1. See Chapter 22 for more details

SOURCES

George Fraser Black, *A calendar of cases of witchcraft in Scotland, 1510–1727* (1938)

David Cook, Ed., *Annals of Pittenweem: being notes and extracts from the ancient records of that burgh, 1526–1793* (1867)

Charles Kirkpatrick Sharpe, *A historical account of the belief in Witchcraft in Scotland* (1884)

Gavin Turreff, *Antiquarian gleanings from Aberdeenshire records* (1859)

THE MONSTRUOUS REGIMENT OF WOMEN
JOHN KNOX PULPIT SPEECH 1558

> It is a thing repugnant to the order of nature that any woman be exalted to rule over men. For God has denied unto her 'the office of a head'. The nobility of Scotland and England are not only subjects to women but slaves to Satan.

This speech was given when the heads of both England and Scotland's Monarchy were queens. Queens who through their own Parliaments would engage with the Witchcraft Act in 1563, and from this the killing years began.

John Knox was leader of the Reformation in Scotland and founder of the Presbyterian Church; he shaped the demographic form of the Government of Scotland and was the author of "The first blast of the trumpet against the monstrous regiment of women", an outspoken attack on the rule of women and their association to the Devil. He personally oversaw some Witch trials in St Andrews, and in later life would be accused of Witchcraft himself when marrying a 17 year-old; he being 33 years older!

CHAPTER 1

ANSTRUTHER WESTER PARISH, 1643
THE ANSTRUTHER "STORM MAKER" WITCH EPPIE LAING

The postcard above was taken in 1870 from the beach at Anstruther in Fife, showing both the parishes of Anster Wester and Anster Easter in the foreground. Both are separated by the width of a burn that runs betwixt them. In this area in 1643, some Witches, two from the locality, were brutally put to death, fixed by ropes to a standing pole with fish barrels full of combustibles placed beneath them; the bodies burnt black to a cheering crowd, the souls of the two already released. They were at least granted strangulation before the fires were lit. This story could be told a hundred times in a hundred villages, the rhetoric is so similar in its ignorance. All it needed was a disaster like crop failure, infant mortality, serious illness, animal ailments, or in this case from the Fife coast village of Anstruther… a shipwreck!

On this spot of beach looking seaward, you can view the two sea islands: the monoliths of the May Island and the Bass Rock, both 5 miles away. The May Island is a mile in length by a quarter mile wide; the Bass about half a mile in length. Both are nothing today but bird sanctuaries with the May Island open to tourists and several boats a day heading out towards its harbour rammed with birdwatchers. Get the weather right and the island can be a terrific venture, which in my family was once a yearly excursion. Basking seals litter the rocks in the sun, bathing like huge, fat sausages; dolphins can be seen, and a host of sea birds over the centuries have bleached the islands white with guano! In all, there's much for the tourists to enjoy if you catch the weather right!

There was once a religious retreat on the May with a village and small church Abbey with hundreds of Monks making a regular pilgrimage to the area. It was ransacked and completely destroyed by several Viking invaders in the year 841. Afterwards, many Scottish kings used to regularly visit the isle to give respect to the many Saints who lost their lives in the Viking invasions.

In days gone by, both islands were treacherous areas for shipping; from a detailed inventory of shipwrecks from 1745–1980, it gives twenty-seven wrecks in the immediate area with a terrible loss of life. Ships travelling into the Forth, heading to the ports of Leith or Pittenweem, had to navigate around the two islands, but by night it was a deadly gamble. For this reason, lighthouses were the step forward to at least try to prevent such calamities in the future. A charter was given from King Charles I in April 1636 to the Earl of Dirleton (James Maxwell), who had a castle rather near to the May Island at North Berwick, a small boat ride away south of the May Isle. The charter was to build a stone lighthouse.

The island was owned by Alexander Cunningham of Barns, and he conceived the design of the lighthouse for his son John and the Earl Maxwell to levy dues for its maintenance. Four shillings per tonne in weight of the ship was deemed a fair levy against ships benefiting from the light it would give. Considering the amount of traffic, it helped—£280 was raised in a year.

The structure, once finished, resembled an old border keep; forty-feet in height with a crude metal basket on the top filled with coal, burning over a tonne a night. A simple pulley system brought coal to the basket, and it was manned by three attendants who lived in the structure with their families. The light survived for a hundred and fifty years but was much complained about by the captains who needed it; they said it was never bright enough to see from afar. Not long after its build, the original architect Alexander Cunningham came to grief in a boat with others not far from the Anstruther coastline. It was just by pure chance that very day, Eppie (Epiphany) Laing stood on the

Billowness area with her friend Isobel Dairsie. They stood in the wind, watching the small fishing craft come to grief in the sprawl of the sea.

The church elders of the town discussed the tragedy. Alexander Cunningham had been a popular man, but all the talk was about the strange storm that blew to the man's destruction, a storm that was ferocious at sea but on the Anstruther coastline was a somewhat peaceful day. Maleficent forces were whispered about over the next few years, and Witches' work was blamed.

Then several witnesses came forward to point the finger at Eppie and her friend Isobel Dairsie who had been seen by others standing watching as the tragic events unfolded in the sea. They were at first accused by the Anster Wester Parish and put in the tolbooth jail; under torture, another Witch from the nearby fishing port of Crail was found... Agnes Wallace. All were now taken to the parish of Crail where further confessions were gained. A confession from Agnes Wallace still exists:

> At the Burgh of Crail, the penult day of October 1643, in the presence of Agnes Wallace being in hand a Witch, was asked how long since she entered the Devil's service, she answered she thought four and forty years being witched by her mother the deceased Margaret Wood.

Margaret Wood had been found guilty of Witchcraft in Crail in 1621 when Agnes was 20 years old. An old trial note from 30 January gives the information:

> Commission to Learmonth of Balgonie and others to try Margaret Wood in Crail suspected guilty of Witchcraft and whose guilt seems established by many pregnant presumptions, likelihood and circumstances in her trial

To the modern eye, this may seem strange, a mother and child having different surnames, but it wasn't until 1822 before females in marriage took the husband's surname. Until then a new child once christened took the father's name, the mother keeping the maiden name.

I can find no date to the arrest of Eppie Laing and Isobel Dairsie, but by August 1643, the St Andrews Presbytery had become involved, sending delegates to delay the execution of Witches… "It is thought fitting, that ministers within the Presbytery do advertise the Presbytery before any Witches with them be put to execution."

With this request, there may have been some questioning to the legality of the women's imprisonment or the length of time in jail already spent! The sea accident was in 1636, seven years before. There is a short note in the St Andrews Parish records from October 11th, 1643, asking for: "Advice on how Isobel shall be used in meat, drink sleep, bed and the like." What the parish was asking was, 'how is she going to pay her jail bills!' The minute you entered jail, you cost money! And the victim, when eventually accepting the penalty to their crime, would have to also settle a bill for their stay in jail.

When the Delegation arrived in Anster Wester Parish from St Andrews, they seemed fairly satisfied with the evidence already on offer from the two Witches' confessions, and they were burnt almost immediately on the Billowness coastline of Anstruther. Then the St Andrews delegation made their way to Crail, five miles distant, and saw to the burning of Agnes Wallace. The historian C. J. Lyon in his *History of St Andrews* states, "that in a matter of a few months, over 40 burnings were observed along the Fife coastline concerning Witches." In my own research for the year 1643 in Fife alone, I can find a great number of trials in the parish records. My count is forty-seven.

> Dunfermline... 19
> Culross... 7
> Anstruther... 2
> Crail... 6
> St Andrews... 4
> Pittenweem 5
> Markinch... 1
> Kinghorn... 2

Isobel Dairsie and Eppie Laing both perished on the Billowness by the laws of the Church at the very place they had witnessed the sea tragedy. We know by the St Andrews Parish interrogation, that Isobel would have trouble paying her jail bills, so she was not a wealthy patron of the village. Not much is said about Eppie Laing, but for years her house was pointed out to tourists till it warranted its own street name, "Witches Wynd". The house still stands today down near the seafront a few hundred yards from the Billowness area. It's a narrow street with what was originally three stone bungalows (one now has an upper floor extension) now holiday homes, the proprietors knowing nothing of the street's notorious history.

This would not be the last case of Witches to meet the flames in Anstruther. Another unfortunate called Elizabeth Dick was burned in April 1701, this time from the east side of the town—Anster Easter parish.

Three years later, the town of Pittenweem had its infamous Witch hunt involving nine accused. One was called Janet Horsbourgh. Although she had a husband in the town, she refused to live with him, staying in accommodation in Anstruther. This was mentioned in the many letters that were written about her treatment under the Pittenweem Parish Council that tried the Witches. "Why was she tried and tortured as a Witch in Pittenweem... when she was living in Anstruther?" The Easter/Wester kirks should have tried her, not Pittenweem parish.

SOURCES

Bob Baird, *Shipwrecks of the Forth and Tay* (2008)

George Fraser Black, *A calendar of cases of witchcraft in Scotland, 1510–1727* (1938)

Rev. J. Dickson, *Emeralds chased in gold; or the Islands of the Forth: their story, ancient and modern* (1899)

John Ferguson, *Bibliographical Notes on the Witchcraft Literature of Scotland* (1897)

George Gourlay, *Anstruther: Or Illustrations of Scottish Burgh Life* (1888)

Rev. Charles Jobson Lyon, *History of St Andrews, Episcopal, Monastic, Academic, and Civil; Comprising the Principal Part of the Ecclesiastical History of Scotland, from the Earliest Age Till the Present Time* (1843)

Stuart MacDonald, *Witches of Fife Witch-hunting in a Scottish Shire, 1560–1710* (2014)

John Stuart, Ed., *Records of the Priory of the Isle of May* (1868)

John Leighton, "Lighthouse on May", *History of the County of Fife* (1840) p. 104

CHAPTER 2

AYRSHIRE PARISH, 1576
BESSIE DUNLOP AND THE GHOSTLY ADVISOR

Going through the Witch trial documents, you can easily run into difficulties with your research for several reasons. Some early trials are written in a mish-mash of Scots dialect and Latin combined, which is where I must refer to past translators and trust their translating as my own ignorance in the language is profound. Our next case is from the courts of Ayrshire, where I must accept the written statements from witnesses to a trial in the Barony of Dalry in 1576. It's an utterly unique case, written in Scots (but translated into English here) and extremely detailed.

In the many cases I have come across to frustrate me with the lack of details, it's the utter contempt shown in Witch Trials to the convicted wretch on trial that stalls research. Sometimes the Courts give the date of the trial, some words describing "some Witches" and the fatal word "umquhill", which means "dead, as in executed"! Sometimes that's all that tells the story of several women or men being tried and convicted by a parish court and the victims burnt to death. Their history is, sometimes if we are lucky, collected by witnesses at the trial or burning and written as diary events or in letters to others, which when matched to the scant court date and execution date, can give a terminated Witch a bit more history with a name and the supposed crime.

This next case is remarkable for its detail and the date

of the trial, just 13 years after the Mary Queen of Scots Witchcraft Act in 1563 made the hunts have a Royal seal to their convictions. We are extremely lucky that we have such information written in English on such an early trial, and what an interesting one it is...

8th November, Lynn, Ayrshire Trial of Elizabeth (Bessie) Dunlop:

Elizabeth Dunlop, spouse to Andrew Jack, living in Lynn in the Barony of Dalry, Ayrshire, was in court on the charges of,

> Dilatet (accused) of using Sorcery, Witchcraft and Incantations with invocating spirits and the Devil. Continually in familiar situations with them at all times. Dealing with charms and abusing the people with said charms and Devilish craft of Sorcery for years past!

Elizabeth was known to have knowledge of things that had been lost or stolen and also helped sick people. She admitted she had no art or science to do such things, only her unique gift was that the dead could indeed converse with her and discuss things she asked!

One such phantom visitor to Elizabeth was Thomas Reid. Thomas (in life) had been a soldier who had met his end in 1547 at the ill-fated Battle of Pinkie Cleugh in Musselburgh near Edinburgh, where the Scottish army under Lord Arran was bested by the English under Edward Seymour, who attacked the Scots forces by sea and land. Thirty ships bombarded the Scots positions, and archery and land cannon decimated the Scots pikemen, who had no answer to the barrage and collapsed in ruins. The Scots leaders escaped from this disaster, but the common man who was ushered into the regiments of spearmen had no defence against cannon and archery except in flight, which was the only escape. Hundreds were cut down by the English and their thousands of mounted horsemen.

Bessie in court, was asked "what kind of man was he?" She replied, "he was an honest and elderly man, grey bearded, and had a grey jacket with sleeves of the old fashion. Grey trousers and stockings above the knee—a black bonnet with silk laces drawn down the folds."

The court continued to ask questions: "How old and in what manner of place did the said Thomas Reid come to her?" Her answer: "As she was going between her house and the yard of Monkcastle, making her way to the pater field to lament as her cow had just died, and her husband and only child were deathly ill with the plague!"

The ghost said, "Good day Bessie?" She replied, "God speed you goodman!" He continued, "Bessie why make you so sour and crying on this day?" Bessie answered, "Have I not great cause to cry? For how money had dwindled away, and my husband and bairn on the point of death. Have I naught cause to have a sore heart?" "Bessie, thow has provoked God and have done something you shouldn't have. You have to mend your ways for your bairn will die and the cow, but your Husband will mend." Thomas then bade her "farewell" and walked away. Next meeting, he asked if she would trust in him. She declared that she would. Thomas then promised her "horses and goods of value if she would deny her Christianity and her faith." She answered: "I would be dragged by horses before doing that, but promised to trust in him."

This rebuke made him angry! He grasped her and took her to an area where there was a kiln for roasting Malt where he forbade her to speak. There were twelve persons; eight women and four men dressed as gentlemen. The women wore plaids and demanded if "she knew any of them". She answered she "knew only Thomas". She was asked "if she would go with them?" She replied "no!" Whereupon they all disappeared with a "hideous rushing sound". She lay frightened and sick till Thomas came again.

The jury asked, "what type of persons were they?" She then said "they were good Witches that dwelt in Elfhame."[2] She told the court that although they asked her to go with them she never went because there was no profit in going and she couldn't leave her sick husband!

Bessie Dunlop now had witnesses come to declare in court that Bessie had a natural gift for curing sick animals, mainly cows and sheep. There was a record of her curing a sick child, and she was renowned as giving out herbs and potions to friends who were sick. One gave evidence that, "she put herbs in her cow's mouth and it did get much better." More evidence gave her skills as a healer, "she helped John Jack's bairn and the Wilson's. And her husband's sister's sick cow!"

She explained to the court: "Thomas Reid had given her herbs from his own hand three times" with which she healed Lady Johnston's servant's daughter. This led to Lady Kilbowye elder, asking if she could mend her leg "which

---

2. Elf-home, fairyland

was crooked". Bessie asked her ghostly friend Thomas Reid who said, "the leg would never mend and only get much worse!" Many more women came with ailments, but Bessie could do nothing without consultation with Thomas. She said that without him she was clueless.

Bessie said that many people would come to her for information about things that had been stollen from them. When asked for examples, she said Lady Thirdpart, Baron of Renfrewshire,[3] asked her "who had stolen her two horns of gold and a crown of gold[4] out her purse?" Bessie took the request to Thomas Reid, and he told her who had taken them... Lady Thirdpart confronted the thief and did indeed get them back.

With the success of Lady Thirdpart getting her possessions back, Lady Blaine then asked about "clothes stolen from her". Lady Blaine was convinced it was one of her servants, but after Bessie spoke to Thomas Reid it was discovered that Margaret Symple, her friend, who had taken them. Another dignified man gave evidence. William Kyle, Burgess of Irvine, asked her "who had stolen his cloak?" A servant called "Malye Boyde" was the answer, but not before she claimed the garment had been altered from a cloak to a skirt. The garment was found at the thief's house and indeed was now a skirt for his wife.

Bemused with these startling examples of Bessie's talents, the court officer asked her "what she thought of the

---

3. Lady Thirdpart was the Baron of Renfrewshire after the death of her husband Hon. William Sempill in 1576. He was the Sheriff-Depute of Renfrewshire.
4. French coins

new faith" when she damned herself answering, "Thomas had said the new faith was no good and the old (catholic) faith should come home again." The Officer then asked "if she had had carnal knowledge with Thomas Reid." She answered, "No, but he would take her to Elfhame." When asked if "she knew that Thomas had died at the battle of Pinky?" and she was recorded answering, "she never knew him in life but he did bade her to go to his son who was Tom Reid (officer to the Laird of Blair) and certain other kinsmen of his and bade then restore certain goods and mend other offences that they had done."

Bessie had delivered herself to the court's justice, and although most of her evidence was in the helping of others through illness or repossessing stolen items, the court couldn't accept the fact that this deity Thomas Reid from Elfhame had corrupted her. She was sentenced to be guilty of Witchcraft and practising sorcery. There was only one outcome for this crime, and she was sentenced to burn at the stake.

Sources

Robert Chambers, *Domestic Annals of Scotland* (1859–61) p.107–110.

George Black, *Calendar of cases of Witchcraft in Scotland* (1938)

Thomas Wright, *Narratives of Sorcery and Magic, from the most authentic cases.* (1851)

Sir Walter Scott, *Demonology and Witchcraft* (1830) p.146.

CHAPTER 3

THE BRECHIN WITCHES

Brechin is a town in Angus, a farmers market town with a cathedral that should give it city status. But the small population spread over a large farming community gives the area a more village or town feel. Nearby lies Forfar, a similar farming town, which is more famous for its Witch trials. However, in the parish records, Brechin has registered many more trials than its neighbour. Their brutality here was astonishing, with actual Witches on record as being burnt alive. I give the details below...

In 1608, The Earl of Mar declared to Brechin Council that he had found several Witches within the town's boundary, and their cases were ready to report to an Assize court. He admitted they were all maintaining their denial of the charges against them. Although torture never changed their pleas, the Earl and his delegates soon came to "guilty" charges against them.

The Earl of Mar was John Erskine, a politician born around 1558. He had succeeded to the Earldom in 1572 and had been guardian to King James VI in the King's youth. The Witches, with their non-stop protestation of innocence, received in return great cruelty from this man.

In the many trials I have information from, occasionally the term "brunt quick!" appears. This term "brunt" is Old Scots speak for "burnt". It signifies the victim was not, as was normal procedure in a witch trial, put to death by strangulation before the actual burning. In this instance in Brechin, the victims were made to suffer the indignity of being burnt alive at the stake!

We shall see this detail again in the Dornoch chapter. While the reason behind this in Dornoch was because the combustion of the materials gathered threatened the executioner before he could finish his job of strangulation, here in Brechin it was simply for cruelty.

The report on this execution in Brechin 1608 states:

> They were brunt quick after such a cruel manner, that some of them died in despair, renounced, and blasphemed and others half burnt, did break out of the fire, and were cast quickly back in again until they were burnt to death!

The names of the burned are never given nor how many were actually in custody. Did the Earl give the command to burn them alive simply because they wouldn't confess? He shared the King's interest in Witchcraft and was a very close friend who was awarded the position of Lord High Treasurer of Scotland in 1615. King James VI is well known as a vigourous prosecutor of Witchcraft, and it is likely his friend and gaurian shared his fervour.

Further cases followed in later years.

In 1619... Marion Marnow was mentioned as a Witch, and that she was "recently burnt."

1620... Sept 30, Andro Tailyeour confessed to being, "guilty of the detestable and devilish crime of Witchcraft, sorcerie and other devilish practices and wicked abuses." His judgement was to burn.

1649... A church sermon by a Mr Thomas Couper

emphasized, "the suspicion of papistry and witchcraft in the parish." With this prompting they found Jonat Coupar in November, who was accused of Witchcraft and executed.

The minister's speech created a witch hunt, and by early 1650 the council could hardly fit its accused witches in the jailhouse: Catherine Skair, Catharin Walker, Elspit Gray, David Mitchel, Alex Coullie, Elspit Erskyn, Alex Hill, Marat Barnett, Thomas Barnett, Marat Melvill Catharin Lyall and Marat Marchant, John Shanks, Thomas Kyneir, John Chrystison, Isobel Reamy, Thomas Bowman, Alex Davidson, Isobel Fordell and Janet Couper.

The trials for witchcraft started by January 3rd and would continue for the year at great expense to the council.

It had all started with Marat Marchant and her husband James Clerk, who had visited David Crystie in Balfield. David later became seriously ill. He gave a death bed confession before the minister, that Marat Merchant was to blame for his illness. It seems David Crystie had taken over the lease of their house, and the pair refused to leave the occupancy of the building. Eventually evicted, they found another house near to him. Because of their eviction, they continually made life unpleasant for David Crystie. At one point, when David was out cutting turfs of Peat for fuel, Marat faced him, looked broadly in his face, "and blew at me where I immediately became sick, so I was not able to leave the house again and have remained sick since."

David had tried to mediate with Marat and James Clerk for taking their house. He had asked to be forgiven, but they had responded with curses and threats. Another witness called John Webster came forward to say that Marat Merchant came to his Mill to grind some corn. He was otherwise busy and could only refuse the job as the millstone needed fixing. Three men could not lift the stone from the floor as Marat sat watching. But as soon as she left the building it was lifted with ease!

On the 17th of January the court sat, and the growing evidence was gathered. Thomas Humble mentioned that two of his cows ate part of Marat's thatched roof on her house… they both later died! Thomas Smyth claimed that Marat had been to his backdoor where he kept his three cows; they all "then produced milk that was loathsome!" Thomas Smart came forward to exclaim she bothered his chickens! David Low said his friend who had promised to help him in the field couldn't make it to work, as he had met Marat Merchant the day before and was now bedridden and sick. Isobel Nachtie had her husband borrow a broom from Marat to sweep up the cattle stables; that night a newly born calf died!

On the 19th of March 1650, Marat Merchant confessed before witnesses that she had met with the devil in the common muir of Brechin and had coupled with him there. She had renounced her baptism and the devil had given her a new name "Jonat Archbald". She pleaded guilty to all the acts put against her and was guilty of David Chrystie's death by blowing in his face. All was confessed to William Alexander the school master and the Baillies.

With the confessions, friends of Marat were also accused. Catherine Skair, Marat Merchant, Catherin Lyall and Jonat Couper were put to the fire. Thomas Humbell and Isoble Fordell were charged with consultation with the witch Marat Gold (who is never mentioned again). Their outcomes are not mentioned; they were most likely banished.

A further trial in 1659 had Janet Sym examined but the evidence against her was very weak.

Recently, a memorial was put up in Inch Park in Brechin to some of the Brechin Witches who suffered.

SOURCES

Extracts from the Presbytery of Brechin from 1639–1660.

Black, *History of Brechin, 2nd ed* p.73.

Register of the Privy council. v.12 p.362

CHAPTER 4

THE BUTE WITCHES, 1632–1673

Rothesay Castle sits by the sea on the island of Bute, by the Rothesay bay—a tall, commanding keep of a castle with history going back to the 12th century and the Norsemen invasions. It has had a troublesome history, its tenancy being interrupted by sieges and violence. Vikings and English invaders have had brief stays here before Scots forces ousted them. Civil wars took their tolls with changing allegiances before the building became a burden in costs to repair. It was finally gifted to the state in 1951 by John Chrichton Stuart, the last owner.

The castle is one of the few remaining today that still boasts a moat with a walkway over it leading to the main entrance. The castle had four defensive towers, then in the

15th century, a large tower and gatehouse was added. There is a trapdoor dungeon in the vaulted passage from the main entrance, more of a windowless pit than anything. From here to the story, we now meet some of the poor creatures that spent their last miserable days on this earth in this dark forbidding cold room: the Witches of the Isle of Bute!

The first such mention of Witches on the island is from the Privy Council records from 1632. It mentions that "several persons accused of Witchcraft, have been lately apprehended." These 'several persons' are never named in any records and seem to have languished in the pit cell where they were dumped. We find more information about them from statements given during the Witch hunt of 1662, where evidence being given against Margaret McWilliam says, "She was delated by confessing Witches from 1632 who died in Prison on the Castle of Rothesay."

It is from this text found in the charter room of Rothesay Castle, all 28 pages of it, that the history of the Bute Witches is laid bare. The 1632 Witches were confessed (through torture?) and generally badly treated to the point they all starved to death in the jail.

1649... Another Witch was found on May 29th, Margaret McKirdy. She was accused of using charms "for the evil eye" and a charm once written in native Gaelic in the register translates as:

> I will put an enchantment on the eye, From the bosom of Peter and Paul, The one best enchantment under the sun, That will come from heaven or earth.

Two men were ordered to stay and observe her and

learn more of her devilish ways and report it at the next session. But no record states what happened to her!

Another brief mention is in the records for 1650, where Findwell Hyndman is "bruited for a Witch". 'Bruited', I presume, is the process of torture applied to the victim. Again, little more addresses what happened to this person. Again in 1661, Jean Campbell was pulled before the Presbytery for "frequenting the company of spirits". Nothing more is mentioned, but the parish was now on a Witch hunt footing as the next year things really heat up!

1662... May 7th, a commission was asked to bring to trial Jonet McIlmartin, Issobel McCan, Margaret McIllivein, and Margaret McWilliam, all from Bute. All had already been processed by torture to confess themselves guilty of Witchcraft.

The 1662 case starts around a sensational sex scandal! The maidservant girl of master Robert Stewart of Scarrell is found unmarried and with child. The finger is pointed at a man in the village, Alexander Bannatyne, but the evidence just doesn't add up. Nancy Throw gives birth on Feb 5th, 1661, when the real father makes himself known. It's none other than the fully respected, university trained, son of Reverend Patrick Stewart of Rothesay parish... Robert Stewart of Scarrell! A fully trained minister himself and a married man.

This is an age of the Church courts having ultimate powers, persecuting with severity such aspects in society as fornicators. Punishments dished out to such sinners would result in brandings, stocks, jail terms, and banishments! Robert held a position as Head Teacher at the local school.

He was thrown out in disgrace from his position, shunned by society for his lying, and banished from his own parish church.

As a fully trained minister, Robert saw a way around his disgrace by holding his own sermons in the hillside. He was a much more vigorous preacher than what his own parish had. A few sermons later, to the horror of his elders who had banished him, Robert Stewart started to get numbers listening to his vibrant speeches. The parish had to act quickly to address the problem. A local farmer and, as it happens, an Elder of the Kirk (another) Robert Stewart of Mecknoch, complained to the parish that the meetings were above his farm on the moor. He called them secret meetings.

Before long a young girl, Janet Morrison, was brought from one of these meetings and told the parish elders of meeting the Devil. This was supported by Margaret McIllivein (McLevin). The parish now decided to arrest the members of the secret meeting.

Margaret McIllivein (McLevin) of Ardroseadale, Jonet Morrison of Kilmory, Issobel McNicoll, and Margaret McWilliam were all arrested, the charge stated, "they had removed themselves from the Presbytery of Scotland and had met in secret meetings." To make matters worse, the women all confessed to the minister of "Robert Stewart of Scarrell using them for sex and promising them rich rewards if they agreed."

Panic set in the parish, with so many accusations and finger pointing it is near impossible to keep up with who was pointing the finger at whom:

Kirstine Ballantyne was wronged by Witchcraft!

Peter Gray bewitched Lady Kames who was delated by Jonet Morisone.

Jonet Boyd was delated by MacArthur for stealing his wife's breast milk!

Katherine Cristell was delated by McLevin as was Katherine Frissel for attending Witch meetings.

Marione Frissell was delated by Jonnet McIlmertine as was Mary Frissell.

Elspat Galie was delated by Jonnet Morrison.

Hew Boyd, who had outlived four wives and one child, was accused as being present at Witch meetings.

John Galie was delated as a Witch also by Jannet Morrison.

Annie Heyman was delated by McLevin who danced at Witches' Sabbaths.

Amy Hyndman was delated by Jonet McIllmertine.

Jonat McConachie was accused of taking the life of a horse and attending meetings…

It goes on and on in this bickering manner, adding many more names for the most trivial of things.

Robert Stewart was humiliated and disgraced and excommunicated but still listed as married to Jean Colquhoun in 1655; she was recorded as married to him in 1673 when his name was mentioned in the parish records. He had been a Schoolmaster.

Margaret McWilliam, Katherine McIllmartin, Jonnet Morison, and Margaret McIllivein were all accused and found guilty of Witchcraft… all burned at "Gallows Craig", a basalt rock beneath the shadow of St Bride's chapel. Four holes had been driven into the rock to take the four stakes. One other, Issobel McNichol, had died in prison due to the tortures and condition of the jail. One other woman called Jonet McNicholl managed to escape the jail and go on the run for 12 years... foolishly she made her way home, hoping the scandal had died down, but once recognised, the sentence of death was re-enacted upon her, and she paid the highest price for coming home!

SOURCES

George Fraser Black, *A calendar of cases of witchcraft in Scotland, 1510–1727* (1938)

William Scott, *The Bute Witches History, Reconstruction of Events, Historical Records and Inferences* (2007)

Highland papers vol. iii, Scottish History Society second series vol. xx, papers relating to Witchcraft 1622–1677

CHAPTER 5

A STRANGE LITTER OF KITTENS IN CAIRNEY

Botarie parish lies on the Aberdeenshire/Banff border. It's been a parish since 1226. The nearby Parish of Ruthven was incorporated into this parish in 1618, and then Botarie/Botriphnie parish became Cairney parish in 1713. Since 1974, the Parish of Cairney has been incorporated itself into a private residence and is a parish no more! That's three churches since 1226 eaten by bigger parishes until sold off completely to private owners.

It's when the parish was named Botarie/Botriphnie that a case before the parish session court in 1654 takes our interest, and what a peculiar case it was. Botarie had found Witches in its borders in 1637, 1643, and 1644. Most, when charged, had fled the area. A woman called Issobell Malcolme was charged on three occasions, but nothing exists to tell of her fate. And this brings us to our most interesting case…

22 March 1654, Botarie parish Court Sessions...
Jean Symson has been compelled to face the session commissioners and Presbytery on three charges:

1. Being accused she had cats in her belly!
2. For approaching the minister of Rothiemay to give her a recommendation for a physician in Aberdeen to give her a medicine to kill the cats in her belly!
3. For approaching Annas Bain, a notorious suspect Witch, on the 7th of February to procure a potion that would kill the cats she had in her belly.

Jean Symson was quite promiscuous. It hadn't gone unnoticed among the young lads of the borough that a roll in the hay was on the cards if you could buy her favour! This was a very dangerous procedure. If loose mouths talked of the act, it wouldn't be long before the parish got heed of it, and that came with the harsh penalties handed out from Church courts towards unwedded action in the crime of "Fornication".

Whippings, penance, and huge fines went with the embarrassment of wearing penitence frocks and to be shamed on your knees in front of the congregation or in the stocks for such crimes. Then forced marriage! Let's not forget when this "Fornication" law was enacted in 1563—in Mary Queen of Scots 9th parliamentary sitting—it actually carried the death sentence! But parish courts rarely went that far. Punishment stretched to whatever the Church deemed suitable, and repeated offences would result in banishment.

In this age, women had no official education

whatsoever: the Education Act of 1496 required the first-born sons of Barons and freeholders to be educated in Latin in schools set up by Priests. Women were educated by only their mothers, in sewing and knitting; in 1750, 90% of women were illiterate. It's with this background that girls were married off very young, some as young as 12.

Jean enjoyed the company of many a boy, and sexual encounters with each lad brought her thoughts to why she wasn't pregnant? She took it to mean she just couldn't, and so she carried on enjoying herself with the male attentions. In Jean's ignorance, she had no idea what the signs of pregnancy were, and when she started to show a bulging stomach, she thought keeping cats in her bed at night had been the cause, or she had been bewitched!

She sought to rid herself of the kittens in her belly! As innocent as she was ignorant, she spoke of her anguish to the minister of Rothiemay, then another minister called William Jaffray of Kinedward,[5] who both were repulsed at her request for "a potion to kill the cats in her belly". They both declared it was a bairn, not cats, in there.

She was not convinced about the wisdom of the ministers, and still convinced she had cats in her belly, so she approached a noble wife of the Aredoule estate[6] but then went to the notorious suspected Witch Annas Bain. On the 7th Feb 1654, Annas Bain denied giving the girl a potion

---

5. "Kinedward" is today's village King Edward (Aberdeenshire), 20 miles from Rothiemay.
6. Aredoul estate is mentioned in the parish sessions in the case. It seems this was Ardo Castle, property of the Forbeses in the 17th century. Today it is a two storey building with 18/19th century modifications.

to rid her of the cats in her belly (Annas probably knew she was being watched after Jean visited the first two ministers). It's at this point the Church arrested Jean and brought her forth to the Kirk sessions to interrogate her.

They found that in 1653, from February to September, she had an affair with a boy of 15 years called John Wat and another called Andro Gray.

Jean's mother, Issobell Crichtoun, was called into court where it was found she had accompanied her daughter to the ministers' houses but denied going in to see the Witch Annas Bain. She went shopping instead and knew naught about whether she had gained a potion or not from her. Standing in court, Jean couldn't face her mother for shame!

James Wat's father was called to the session. Alexander Wat had exclaimed the two youths had slept in separate beds under his mill roof on several occasions, and he also had been asked to procure a potion to kill the cats! He was asked by the Presbytery court, "why would he be prepared to kill the cats knowing it was a bairn," knowing his son had slept with her? His answer was, "he could take the fault!"

The court made its declaration on 19 April 1654.

"It Comperit John Wat of fornication with Jean Symson on the first of September last and take the guiltiness of his child!"

James Wat replied to the court that Jean had said she had loads of others before him and hadn't conceived, and to this the court agreed she had indeed thought this... the court suborned him to take the guiltiness.

Jean, at least 8 months pregnant at this time, would have endured a penance charge from the parish and a forced marriage. There is no information as to what sex the bairn was or if they lived happily ever after!

Cats are no stranger to the Witchcraft cases. Many a postcard or Halloween decoration has our typical Witch with broom and of course the obligatory black cat! It all stems from 1232 and the rule of Pope Gregory IX, where he declared that, "cats were evil and associated with the Devil and Witchcraft." We shall see the horrible effects of this proclamation in later chapters.

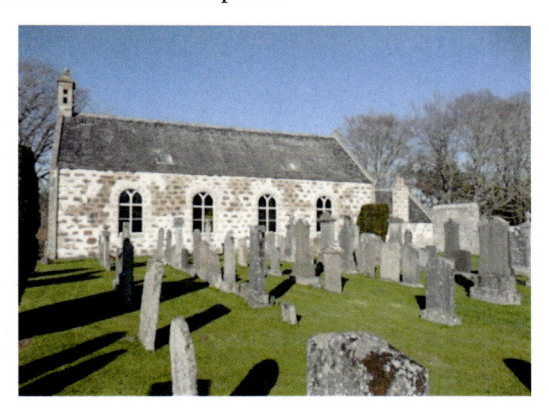

Cairney church as it looks today... now a private residence... once Botarie Parish

Sources

James Frederick Skinner Gordon, *The Book of the Chronicles of Keith, Grange, Ruthven, Cairney, and Botriphnie Events, Places, and Persons* (1880)

Joy Cameron, *Prisons and Punishment in Scotland From the Middle Ages to the Present* (1983)

Martin Coventry, *Castles of Scotland* (2005)

CHAPTER 6

THE CRAIL WITCHES

The Witches Jail At Wormiston Castle

Crail is a most picturesque seaport. It is situated on Fife's most easterly point with direct access to the fertile fishing grounds of the North Sea. Its history is entwined with the violent incursions of the Nordic host. Viking raiders established themselves a stronghold here from the 9th century. Long forgotten battles have outdated their own history, but what is known is the Scottish King Constantine (862–877) met his end here in battle. The son of Scotland's first king, Kenneth MacAlpin, attacked a force of Vikings here that had prepared the ground for defence. It went badly for the Scottish king. A cave near the sea is long in tradition as being the spot where Constantine was beheaded by the Danes. The dead king was taken to Iona Island and laid to rest with his ancestors, Iona being the traditional burial ground of the Kings.

Stone cists for years have turned up in the ploughed fields here, and I remember as a child on the Fife Ness beach cliffs lifting stone slabs that held many human remains underneath. That's all that's left of the Norse encampment and the violence that took place here.

Farming and fishing here go hand in hand with the superstitions that kept the place in fear for hundreds of years. When the parish ministers talked of wrecked boats at sea or failed crops it was always the fault of others. Confusion and ignorance to apprehend the misery and starvation that followed needed answers for "how could it be so?" The ministers provided the act of Witchcraft in the area to remedy the blame. The peculiar, the healer, and the vagabond were sought in big numbers here and destroyed as Witches.

In 1588, a woman in Crail is mentioned in the trial of a Witch in St Andrews called Agness Melville. Agnes had called upon Catherine Pryde living in Crail and administered treatment for a stomach complaint. Herbs of parsley, onions, comfrey, wormwood, elecampane, and cochlearie[7] were mashed into a soup and then drank. It seemed to work. But for Agness Melville, repeating the same cures to the Archbishop of St Andrews had her accused and burnt (her story is in the St Andrews Witches,

---

7. also known today as "scurvy grass".

Chapter 26). Catherine Pryde's fate for supporting a Witch is never mentioned.

Crail's first victim of the Witch trials came two years later in 1590. King James VI was pursuing a huge Witch hunt in North Berwick, over 80 Witches were accused, he personally oversaw the trials and took great interest. With this, his nearest friends and supporters took on their own quests to find and root out Witches in their local vicinities. The parish of Crail found its first victim: Euphame Lochoir. She was held by the parish and transported to St Andrews where the overjoyed ministers wrote in the session, "the Presbytery ordains every minister to try the same as far as they can specialise the session of Crail."

King James VI oversees witch trials. Engraving from his own 1597 book, *Daemonologie*.

Her outcome is not recorded.

In 1599, Geillis Grey was found and jailed by the Crail minister. One of the Lairds thought the Church's treatment was too soft on her. The Laird of Lathocker took her from the jail to his own castle.[8] Completely unsatisfied with the Church's soft approach to torture, he saw to it himself in the comfort of his own dungeons and privacy. He brutalised

---

8. Lathocker Castle was built in 1383 by the Wemyss family. By the 1800s, the castle had been broken down and a mansion house built by the Horsburgh family… by the 1900s, it fell into disrepair, it had a record of poltergeist activity and was deemed unfit to live in… building landscaped in 1970… now nothing exists.

her, maiming her hands with thumbscrews that tightened over the fingers till the bones broke under pressure and the marrow of the fingers bled out! The Laird of Lathocker certainly got his confession, but the Church in Crail complained she would be nothing but a burden to them as a beggar as her hands were so damaged, she could never use them again!

Her outcome was never noted.

In 1620, Margaret Wood was caught. Her accusations in the parish records, "many pregnant presumptions of Witchcraft!" We can ascertain that her guilt was established here since she was burnt in the burgh of Crail. What we know about Margaret Wood is that she had a daughter. Knowledge of this would become clear in another trial 23 years later!

1625 brought Marjory Patterson and one other into the courts to be tried as Witches. No further details exist, but Crail was getting good at burning Witches.

1643, on 16th August, there's mention of a Witch being found. By September 6th, parish records state "some Witches". In turn, in October, we are given a name to one of them… Agnes Wallace. She is mentioned as the daughter of Margaret Wood burned in Crail in 1620! Agnes Wallace was taken to the secure jail cells of Wormiston Castle and held in the dungeons by Patrick Lindsay, the laird. A confession still exists for which Patrick Lindsay was a witness. Agnes had been condemned to Wilmerston jail[9] by Jonnet Inglis, a relative of deceased Thomas Cunyngham and Barbara Balfour. It seems Agnes was accused of their deaths by

---

9. Wormiston castle jail.

Witchcraft. The parish records state casually in October, "some Witches burnt". It seems the unnamed Witch with Agnes Wallace was burned also.

The author has recently been filmed at this location talking to stars of the *Outlander* series about the Crail Witches for *Two Men In Kilts*. The jail today is still in good condition; anyone inside has no means of escape once the door is fastened.

In 1644, Beatie Dote was demanded from Crail to stand trial in the parish court of Pittenweem. She was found guilty and with several others was burnt in the Priory gardens. Bills still exist showing the costs given to the families of the burnt Witches, itemising the ropes and fuel needed to burn them… all bills were paid in full.

The last unfortunate was taken in 1675, Grillis Robertson,[10] whose own daughter testified against her. As at this time there were no Crail baillies at hand; she languished in the jail until one could be found. When one finally made it to the parish, Grillis Robertson was already dead through starvation and ill treatment!

Sources

George Fraser Black, *A calendar of cases of witchcraft in Scotland, 1510–1727* (1938)

John Ferguson, *Bibliographical Notes on the Witchcraft Literature of Scotland* (1897)

---

10. "Grillis Robertson" is original trial records spelling; "Geilles Robertsone" is given by MacDonald and some others.

Stuart MacDonald, *Witches of Fife Witch-hunting in a Scottish Shire, 1560–1710* (2014)

J. E. Simpkins, *County Folk-lore: Fife. Vol 7* (1914)

CHAPTER 7

THE CROOK OF DEVON WITCHES

Tullibole Castle, where in 2013, the resident Lord Moncrieff put up a monument to honour the eleven Witches killed near here in his castle lands. He stated to the press: "It's shocking what happened to these poor people who had done nothing wrong!"

The Crook of Devon was a small village in Perthshire, part of the Parish of Fossaway on the river Devon, 6 miles from Kinross. It has its own Barony and takes its name from the small bend or turn (Crook) in the river near here. The waters are beautifully pure, and they fall into a deep and gloomy chasm, forcing their way down through quaint little humpback bridges where their flow gets most violent until it feathers out into the Forth river. The banks are so steep here, a huntsman pursuing a fox with hounds along the riverbank in 1790, not being too clever on his surroundings, took a wrong turn, losing all his dogs over the cliff edge where they fell to their doom.

The locals, few as they were around here in 1662,

scared by superstition and legend, named this spot "The Devil's Mill", as the water pays no regard to a Sunday and keeps pouring forth. It was this heightened fear of the Devil in these lands that brought so many Witches from such a small population.

The Parish of Fossaway had credit for persecuting and killing a Witch in 1643; Johnne Brughe fell foul to the charges of "dilatit of diverse poyntis of sorcerie" and was burnt on the Castlehill of Edinburgh. Although in the parish lands, it seems the Barony of Montcrieff pursued the Witches of the Crook of Devon in 1662 and tried and killed them within the castle lands. The records of the trial are still intact and very detailed. I give the best of it from the pages of J. E. Simpkins, *County Folk-lore: Fife. Vol 7* (1914), pp.359–373…

> From the Justiciary court records held at The Crook of Devon, 3rd April by Mr Alexander Blair his Majesty's justice Depute general 1662. The persons put on trial are thirteen in number consisting of one Warlock named Robert Wilson and twelve Witches. As thirteen normally forms the organised company of Witches.

> Proceedings against Agnes Murie of Kilduff, Bessie Henderson of Pitfar, Isabel Rutherford from Crook of Devon.
>
> Ye all three are indytit and accusit for as much as by the Divine Law of the almighty God set down in his sacred word especially chapter 18 of Deut, and chapter 20 of Levit made against the users and

practisers of Witchcraft and 22 chapter of Exodus 18 verse... "Thou shalt not suffer a Witch to live" also by the acts of Parliament on the 73rd act of the ninth paliment of our soverign lords great grandmother (Charles II) Queen Mary of good memory.

Bessie Henderson's confession Said Sorcery and Witchcraft that ye being coming from the Crook Mill (named as "The Devil's Mill") about Martinmas last 1661. Satan did appear to you at the bank of the Tullibole, being Monday and said, "will you be my servant and I will give you as much silver as will buy you as much corn as will serve you before Lammas" he renounced your baptism and gave you a new name... "Rossina". Satan had the use of your body and you were at a meeting of Satan with Robert Wilson his spouse Gillies Hutton, Margaret Duncan and Agnes Allen of Devon.

More Witches were named from the three Witches after torture was put upon them... Bessie Henderson, Isabel Rutherford, Robert Wilson, Agnes Pittendreich, Margaret Huggon, Bessie Neil, Margaret Litster, Janet Paton, Agnes Brugh, and Christian Grieve. The rigours of torture were used and poor Margaret Huggon died during the harshness of it. She was 79 years old! All confessed to the charges before long to Mr Alexander Ireland the present minister and Mr Robert Alexander the baillie.

On the 28th March, 1662, Agnes Sharp from Peatrig and Janet Paton of Kilduff were added to the growing trial.

Evidence against the Witches started piling up... Janet Millar spouse to Henry Anderson was sworn in saying,

> Agnes Murie who came to Anderson's house where he was about to bring home his Oxen from the field, suddenly took ill, he was stricken speechless and lost the power of all but one of his sides, he was fourteen days speechless and one year ill.

From the above statement, we can today recognise the man has suffered all the symptoms of a stroke. With no medical knowledge of such things in 1662, it was looked at as Witchcraft and just unlucky that Agnes Murie was there at the time.

More evidence came this time: a farmer called Robert Futt had a horse go down ill followed by several ewes after a visit from the Witch Isabel Rutherford. The Witch Bessie Henderson put a hand on James Wilson ten years back and the man had been ill since! Bessie Henderson said she had been a Witch for forty years in the Devil's service and had met him with Isabel Gibson and Janet Paton in the harvest of 1661.

The confessions came thick and fast, and the Justice Mr Alexander Colville of Blair summed up the trial...

> It is found and declared be the hail Assize all in one voice that the forenamed Agnes Murie is guilty and convict in six out of seven points of Witchcraft and sorcerie and that according to her own free confession as also the said Bessie Henderson is guilty in like manner, the above Isabel Rutherford is guilty

> and convict in points of Witchcraft according to her own confession.
>
> All three to be taken to the place called Cruick Mill for execution tomorrow... 4th April bodies to be burnt to ashes for their trespass.

A second trial found Robert Wilson of Devon, Bessie Neil of Golvin, Margaret Lister of Kilduff, John Paton of Devon, and Agnes Brugh "all guilty in the Devilish trade of Witchcraft. With one voice all are convicted to burn as common sorcerers and notorious Witches by the mouth of Edmond Mercer chancellor of the Assize."

Next came three more trials condemning Christian Grieve, Margaret Hutton, Janet Brugh (Agnes' Sister), Janet Paton, and Margaret Huggon—all to be burnt on the hillock of Lamblaires. Agness Pittendreich escaped sentence as she was pregnant, but she was kept in jail till she gave birth then she was committed to the flames as her sin never involved the innocent, newborn child.

Today the little hillock of Lamblaires sits in a field unmolested by its horrid past; nothing here commemorates the horrors that happened there, but thanks to the Lord Moncrieff, we now have a permanent reminder inside the maze next to the castle; a one and a half tonne block of cut sandstone with five sides, a side for each of the recorded trials with the names of the accused. I raise a glass for Lord Moncrieff and wish there were more like minded councils that could see past Church minister protests to erect more monuments to local people who were murdered by the local parishes.

The monument is the centre piece of a one hundred foot hedge maze, which is a huge hit for the tourists. In my opinion, the Lord Rhoderick Moncrieff has to be admired for the monument; he shames other councils that shy from the idea that Witches are not deserving of lasting tributes.

Sources

The Gazetteer of Scotland, p. 316. (1844)

G. Black, *Calendar of Witchcraft* (1938)

Larner, Lee and McLauchlan, *Source Book of Witchcraft*

J.E. Simpkins, *Country Folklore* (1914)

CHAPTER 8

THE CULROSS WITCH-HATERS

Culross Abbey was converted into a parish church in 1560, after the Reformation. Half the Abbey has been left to go to ruin, but the steeple was used as a jail for the many Witches found in this little town.

Culross, on the west coast of Fife, is so typical of the sea towns and villages across this coastline. It has the traditional narrow streets and old stone built 300– to 400-year-old houses with remarkably small doorways (the bigger the doorway the more you had to heat the house!). There's always a proud parish church standing tall in these little fishing villages as there is one here. It was an Abbey run by Monks, but incorporated into a parish during the Reformation of 1560.

Culross also has a tolbooth, which governs the four square miles that hold the population. The tolbooth was built in 1625, when Culross was a rich, busy haven of a place. It once had fifty salt pan houses down by the beach, houses designed for the extraction of seawater then boiling it down in huge metal pans; once boiled dry, the sea salt could be scraped into bags and used to cure fish in barrels. It was a costly process. It took burning about 5 tonnes of coal to make 1 tonne of salt; but having a prosperous coal mine in the little town, everything depended on each other to profit. The fishermen needed salt, the salt needed coal, and the coal had to be dug out from the mine. Jobs for all!

Having a population of around six hundred in 1625, the tolbooth was built to show a high status community at large. It had a council chamber for its baillies and now a jail... but the year the tolbooth was built was the year everything collapsed in on itself. In 1625, a massive storm washed away the stone works protecting the deep mine, it flooded and collapsed, the rich coal seams lost for all time. The salt pans now had to find coal from outside the burgh, which was expensive and slow to get. Gradually, the salt pans numbers reduced, then the fishing fleet left the ruined harbour. All had vanished, but Culross still stood!

It still had spinning industry, but plague and soon civil wars would tear this little place apart further. And with the despair and hardships would inevitably come the accusations of Witchcraft. And boy did they find plenty here! In a sixty year period, thirty named Witches would be found in this little burgh, and another trial giving no names—just "some Witches burnt" (records suggest the number of actual witches found in Culross was 44 in number)—to the history books. When the church steeple jail became too crowded, they started to incarcerate them in the tolbooth.

The Culross tolbooth (original design) was built in 1625, the same year the coal mine flooded. Some rooms here would be used as a jail for the many Witches found in this area. A turret was added with a bell in 1783, and the building was still in use till 1975.

It was 1621 when they found the first Witch in Culross; Christiane Couper, who the council register states, "has confessed said crymes especillie the use of charmes, for the glorie of God and punishment of so hevenous and foul a cryme justice be done upon her". Her outcome is not noted, but the wording of the above suggests they took her crime to the maximum penalty. She was kept in the church steeple where there was a secure room used as a jail.

In 1624, they had a commission granted to try Jonet Umphra in which, from the Privy Council register, it states, "she has confessed the crime and had meetings and conference with the Devil." Jonet under torture confessed to more Witches in the area... Mayse Umphra her own sister, Alex Clerk, Mary Rowland, Marioun Stirk, Jonnet Watt, Helen Ezatt, Jonnet Tor, and Anne Smith from nearby Torryburn. Two of the prominent figures living in the area judged over them, Robert Bruce and John Peaston. Again, there is no outcome to this event, but with such high charges, I presume they never escaped the flames (Robert Bruce would soon be killed fighting a duel). The Witch hunts in the area continued, and through the records we find...

1634... Four women caught and suspected of Witchcraft... no outcome noted. Named as Jonet Dusone, Helen Rowane, Kath Rowane, Grissel Astrin.

1636... Margaret Fields arrested for Witchcraft... no outcome.

1641... William Drysdale accused and suffered public repentance.

1641... another trial, this time Katherine Mitchell was found guilty of Witchcraft and executed.

1643... March 5th... so many women were incarcerated in the church steeple jail on Witchcraft charges that

Catherine Rowan had to be moved to the tolbooth rooms (Kirk session minutes)… "John Waster fined for being soothsayer."

1643… May 14th… Marion Thompson accused by Isobel Eizatt as a Witch (Marion's reputation was well known). The Council papers state "other women being watched."… On the 28th… "Margaret Hutton has ran to Stirling… Suspected of Witchcraft. Marion Burges and Elspeth Shearer also caught."

1644… Beatrix Bruce on 28th Feb… she named three others after torture… outcomes unknown.

1644… Mary Cunningham and her daughter were arrested in August. Some documents are available to see the treatment they received solely because they got an Advocate to file a complaint to the Council as to their hellish treatment. It says…

> She and her daughter had been illegally imprisoned in the Tolbooth of Culross and had been most barbarously treated, very cruelly and inhumanly usit by them under direction of James Kennowie the Clerk. Arrested without a warrant she describes her treatment…
>
> "When they put us in Prison they causit their officers and hangmen to tie us naked, rape and search our bodies and secret members for Witchmarks, and when they found none upon us they put sackclothes gownes upon us and locked our legs in irons and would suffer us no meat or drink to cum in to us by other than the jailor who satisfied his own appetite

with it. Famine and cold brought great misery and sickness to us." [11]

1648... March Margaret Holden arrested of Witchcraft.... Her fate is not recorded.

1649... Janet Paterson arrested.

1650... Robert Cousing arrested.

1656... In June, Elspeth Craiche is apprehended as a Witch in the tolbooth. Edinburgh Parliament refused a commission to try her as a Witch; therefore, the town decided to banish her instead.

1662... unfinished business....Elspeth Craiche is re-arrested, and during her torture, she confessed with unnamed others... they were all burnt in Culross.

1665... "Some witches are recorded as burnt in Culross!"

1675... Four women are accused, three are recorded as Widows, Katherine Sands, Isobel Inglis, Agnes Hendries, Jonet Hendries. All have confessed to carnal copulation with the very Devil himself. All were burnt and the expense for the burning was taken by the sales of their houses and property.

1684... Helen Eliot... It is Helen Eliot that brought my interests to Culross as her treatment was basically very cruel. Not much exists of her accusations, but letters written in 1684 by a man who witnessed her burning describes her story:

---

11. It is obvious that Mary Cunningham was of some wealth to afford the services of a lawyer; he must have been good as there is no more written about the case.

I had the curiosity, when I was a scholar to pass over from Borrowstonness to Culross to see a notable Witch burnt. She was carried out to her place of execution in a chair by four men, by reason her legs and her belly were broken, by one of the Devil's cunning tricks which he plaid her. This woman was watched in the steeple of Culross, by two men, John Shank and John Drummond, who being weary went to another room where there was a fire to take a pipe. To secure her she had her legs put in stocks and locked into them. No sooner were they out the room when the Devil came for her. He embraced her and carried her away out of the prison at which she exclaimed "oh god where are you taking me!" and at this, the Devil dropped her where she broke both legs and her belly. It is said the imprint of her heels was left in the grass for many years and brought many tourists to the area to see.

Obviously, this was the guard's story to save them getting into trouble for not watching her properly. A beauty of a story it was. With a bit of detective work, you can see the window she may have jumped from, and it would be a sore landing for her if she still had the leg restraints on. As for "break her belly" she may have suffered stomach trauma in her escape, hitting a wall in her desperate escape. What is sure was her last hours on this earth were extremely painful, lifted by four men to a waiting burning pyre, with two broken legs and holding her own intestines in. Death, I imagine for her, couldn't come quick enough!

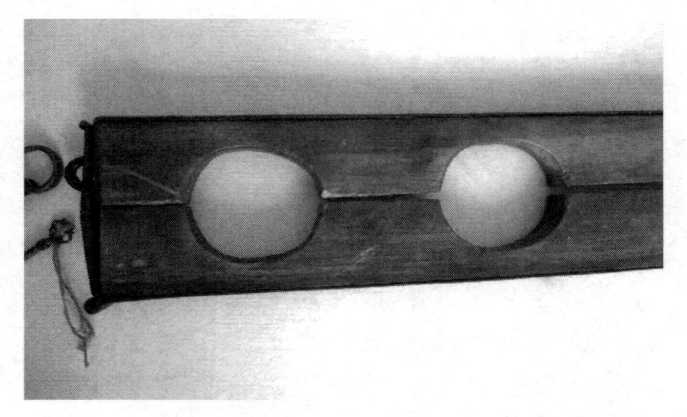

Wooden stocks used to keep Helen Eliot in the church steeple jail. Did she jump from the steeple room still wearing the apparatus breaking her legs and splitting her stomach?

Sources

David Beveridge, *Culross and Tulliallan, Or Perthshire on Forth Its History and Antiquities... from the Burgh and Kirk-session Records* Volume 1 (1885)

GF Black, *A calendar of cases of witchcraft* (1938)

Robert Chambers, William Chambers, *The Gazetteer of Scotland* (1844)

Stuart MacDonald, *Witches of Fife Witch-hunting in a Scottish Shire, 1560–1710* (2014)

James Wilkie, *Bygone Fife, from Culross to St. Andrews. Traditions, Legends, Folklore and Local History of "the Kingdom"* (1931)

CHAPTER 9

THE DEVIL'S HORSESHOE IN DORNOCH

The old tolbooth jail in Dornoch, where Janet Horne and her disabled daughter were held.

Dornoch in 1727 was a ragged poor area. Five hundred people lived the Highland way of existence, toiling small croft lands with minimal produce. Oats, beans, barley, and potatoes were the staples yielded, but the church registered a hundred poor people in its parish lands. Petty feuds and jealousies were rife. Not many spoke English; the native Gaelic was spoken broadly here.

Having several miles of coastline, one would expect a thriving fishing fleet, but it wasn't so—one miserable boat was all that worked from here. The roads were in atrocious condition with a hellish lack of bridges over the rivers. From these conditions came an outdated last vent of persecution towards an old woman and her disabled daughter on charges of Witchcraft. Or in Gaelic… Bhuidseachd.

Some places are aptly named, so much so that future history merges into the fold of the name surreptitiously and without grace. Dornoch, near Inverness in the Highlands, has the claim of the last Witch to be burnt in Britain. The history of the trial is very fragmented; parish records of the event don't exist! Dornoch Parish records don't go further back than 1730—all records have perished with age and the confusion of the Jacobite rebellion that took place here in 1745. The only records we have are from private letters written by bystanders who viewed the horrifying spectacle of the burning. The central courts of Edinburgh did not conduct the trial, leaving it to the jurisdiction of the parish court, so no official records exist of the affair.

A letter from Thomas Woodrow of Eastwood, dated 18th April 1727 to James Frazer of Ross, gives details of it, as does another letter from a Mr Burt whose written work on the North of Scotland was collected and published by William Patterson in 1876. It is mentioned in *The Statistical Account of Scotland* (1793) under the Parish of Loth, which is in the jurisdiction of Dornoch, but it's difficult to get to the source information of the event. Past writers have all written from each other, never investigating properly, which is very lazy. There is a rough stone monument supposedly marking the spot of the burning, but even that has a date on it as 1722, which is wrong as it happened in June 1727, which adds to the confusion. But here is what I have unearthed from my records...

In 1259, in the reign of King Alexander III, the Viking warlords were ransacking the vulnerable coastal towns in Scotland.[12] One army landed in Inverness, where William, Earl of Sutherland was caught unawares. He sent a small force to meet the threat, headed by his kinsman Richard de Moravia. He was to hold them off as best he could till William could muster his main forces. Richard met them full on and fought bravely, buying time with his own life; he was cut down just as his brother joined the battle with his main force. The huge broadswords and axes would leave a field littered with broken bodies and severed limbs from dying men and horses; a field of gore is what it became as the fight was joined, Clansmen to Viking, slaying foes with neither giving ground.

Earl William was looking for the Viking Thane—to kill the general would tip the balance—and there he found him in the middle of the melee. Finally, the two leaders met in a desperate battle and the Danish lord seemed to get the better of William, disarming him, his sword knocked away. With victory in mind, or maybe thinking of a ransom

---

12. Some accounts give the date of the battle as 1245, which would have been in the reign of Alexander II. Date given here taken from *The history of the feuds and conflicts...* (1790).

for his prisoner, the mighty Thane of Denmark hesitated for a moment. William reached out on the ground and his hand found the severed stalk of a horse's leg. He brought the leg down like a mace against the Viking lord's skull, its hoof bearing an iron horseshoe. The weapon was crude but effective as it crushed the enemy's skull! With the loss of their captain, the Vikings could only see to escape, and many were cut down. William had a victory, but the cost was high as many men perished as well as his own kinsman. To commemorate the victory, he gave the place of battle the name of a horse's foot in Gaelic... Dorn-Eich, which in time becomes Dornoch. The town would incorporate the battle into its heraldic badge of honour, bearing proudly a horseshoe as its coat of arms!

From its birth, Dornoch's name came from the humble horseshoe; it's fitting to have the story of the last Witch in Britain destroyed here with a charge of Witchcraft regarding horseshoes also. A ridiculous charge, and it's beyond belief to understand what this woman was accused of and the reasons she died so horribly.

What is said of Janet Horne is that she was an old woman; she had been a maid in her professional life and had worked abroad for most of her years, possibly in Italy. When in her old age, she had come back to her hometown of Dornoch with a disabled daughter, the Parish of Loth had her arrested simply because of her daughter's disability, being deformed club-like feet, by the minister, who was a Mr Robert Robinson.

Clubfoot is a recognised medical term for feet that turn inwards, like one is walking on the sides of your feet, it's not a painful ailment but one's gait would look awkward, and the obvious disablement would bring unwanted attention from suspicious locals.

The charges brought to Janet from the parish was that she had her daughter's feet fitted with horseshoes by the Devil, and she then rode her around the sky. The daughter was seen to have not fully returned to human form: her club feet being seen as hooves—hooves the Devil had fitted iron horseshoes on. Being away from Scotland on foreign shores for many years, she was forced to read the Lord's Prayer in native Gaelic; so long from reading such material, she stumbled over the words, which angered the minister more, and in his eyes, concluded the woman's guilt.

The charges were put forward by Captain David Ross of Littledean who was Deputy Sherriff of Sutherland. Both mother and daughter were put in the tolbooth jail in Dornoch, where somehow the disabled daughter managed to escape out of a window at night.

The charges then carried to the mother, where she was condemned when she was made to recite the Lord's Prayer from the native Gaelic, and she, being unfamiliar with the language simply for being away for so long from the country, mis-quoted the first line. For this mistake, she was sentenced to be burned to death. On her way to execution, the woman's age may conceal what we understand today as Dementia. She was so confused as to the fuss being created around her, she actually stopped and warmed her hands on her own burning pyre, mentioning "it was a bonny fire". She was placed in a tar barrel and hoisted into the flames.

In sad retrospect, this woman's name may not even have been Janet, but it was a derogatory term used as slang for most Witches. It derives from the Middle Eastern name for a spirit "Jinn" sometimes "Jinny". That "Jannet" actually comes from the term "Jenny" because of the similar sounding relationship, the two words bastardise themselves into the slang term "Janet" as a Witch's name. It's no mistake that many went to the flames in Scotland as Witches re-christened by court ledgers as "Janet", and the author's own research finds 262 "Janets" in the Scottish courts on Witchcraft charges (I really should get out more!). It is the most common first name by over a hundred (Margaret comes second with 133).

That's our last Witch in Britain to meet the extreme measures of the courts; we only know scraps about her, we don't know her daughter's name, we may not even have the woman's real name. The memorial even has the wrong date of 1722 on it! But that it actually took place is certain from the letters sent in 1730 by Mr Burt, who witnessed it, giving the proper date. Who did it and when a stone was erected is uncertain, but like the "Maggie Wall" memorial in Perth, it has cast shadows on the correct information.

An interesting footnote in the old *Statistical Accounts of Scotland* show records of Loth parish that state that, "the common people did entertain strong prejustice towards Janet Horne's relatives (her daughter) to this day" (written in 1797).

Sir Walter Scott, in a chapter of his book *Demonology and Witchcraft*, writes in 1830 that, "the Marchioness of Sutherland (Elizabeth Sutherland Gower 1765–1839) did offer protection to the child of the Burnt Witch in which the disabled daughter did produce a son with the same disability. He was under the Marchioness's charity in 1830."

Walter Scott was a great friend to the lady, and his information would have come direct from her. Sir Walter Scott actually met an old man who was present at the burning of Janet Horne as a boy. The man mentioned watching as she, on being walked to her burning fire, warmed her hands on the flames not knowing they were actually for herself. As a footnote, she was burned alive, or as the Scottish parishes sometimes write "brunt quick", as the old man told Sir Walter that her screams haunted him all his natural life.

Today in Dornoch you can still see the stone placed to commemorate Janet Horne's burning place. It actually sits in someone's back garden near to the old golf course. And it's with kind permission from the owners that they will let you come in and observe the memorial and photograph it.

The author with the wrong dated (1722) stone marking the burning spot of Janet Horne.

From a town named for the bloody image of a horseshoe, it shames the image in the persecution of a woman on Witchcraft charges who was reported to have shod her own daughter in horse's shoes.

Although Dornoch claims the last burnt witch, there was another late case on the Island of Skye in 1747. A beggar woman called Mrs MacKinnon was accused of poisoning Ruaridh Mc Iain Macdonald of Armadale's men. To get a confession of witchcraft from her they bound her with ropes and hung her above a fire to burn her feet. The bones of her feet fell apart, burnt to charcoal. She managed to crawl free away from the fire before dying 12 days later. Ian Macdonald can thank the chaos of the aftermath of Culloden for not being charged with murder. Instead, he was charged with the new Government act of being caught wearing tartan! The Dress Act 1746 made wearing tartan illegal, and was punished with 6 months jail sentence then transported to the colonies if a second offence was commited.

Sources

The history of the feuds and conflicts among the clans in the northern parts of Scotland and in the Western Isles (Glasgow: Printed by J. & J. Robertson for John Gillies, Perth. 1780)

Sir John Sinclair, *The Statistical Account of Scotland Drawn Up from the Communications of the Ministers of the Different Parishes* Volume 7 (1793)

G Black *Calendar of Cases of Witchcraft* (1930)

Burts Letters from the North of Scotland (1754) p125

Gazetteer of Scotland vol 1 (1844) p. 323

Inverness court papers, Aug 1754

CHAPTER 10

ISOBEL YOUNG, DUNBAR 1629

Isobell Young was a native of East Barns, a small fishing port in Lothian two miles distant from Dunbar and twenty-eight miles east of the city of Edinburgh. What we know of her is taken from her trial notes. She was middle aged and married to George Smith, and they owned a house on the sea front. That she could at least afford to have her own lawyer for her defence suggests the family did have some resources, but for all the help he gave her, she was just as well to add the money as fuel to her own burning!

In her trial, some of the accusations of Witchcraft were dragged up from nineteen years past. One instance being the mill belonging to George Sandies, where, with a spot of calm weather, it ceased to turn its wheel. The wind driven mill-stone stayed stationary over several days. A nice break in the weather to some folk, but George Sandies was sure it was due to nothing but enchantment. In her trial, the other accusations came thick and fast.

A sickness came over the cattle of William Meslet. They mysteriously took ill, as did his reputation for fishing during the mackerel season when the fish were abundant in massive numbers. Once the fleet was out in the action, his was the only boat that could not get a catch, while the others were filling barrels with fish. It was witnessed and reported in the trial that Isobell, for reasons known only to herself, had taken her clothes off inside a barn and ran round in circles three times! It was said this was her way of putting a curse on the beasts and misery on Mr Meslet's fishing ability.

Isobell Young was seen to walk on water. As it was reported, at high tide she could walk across the waves to her own house on the shore without getting wet, where on this tempestuous night a mill horse following the same route could hardly keep its feet.

She had over time associated with other notable Witches, one being Christian Grinton, who had been watched entering Isobell's house and then exiting via a hole in her roof in the form of a black cat! Then returned in human form again, this time using the front door. Another local woman with an unsavoury reputation as a Witch was Janet Lindsay. She was seen in Isobell's company many times and got the fishwive's tongues all talking about Isobell in questionable company!

A fellow farmer of Dunbar had an argument with Isobell, and she was heard to say, "all would not go well with him…" The consequences of this warning came true when he collapsed and died next day. A fatal heart attack took him while working behind his own plough as he laboured in the field. A Witch Pricker was brought to examine Isobell Young, and before long, he had found what he knew to be "the Devil's mark" on her body.

The judges on the trial called the Laird of Lee to see if the court could use his legendary "Lee penny stone", which was a magical ancient talisman that had reputation for remarkable powers to heal cattle if dipped in their water requirements. The stone has a remarkable history from 1330, and it was thought it could combat the supposed spell put upon the cattle by the Witch. The story of this magical gemstone, although briefly associated with this trial, is remarkably interesting indeed and if the reader may permit me, I leave this trial for a moment to give the history of the said object.

In 1329, King Robert the Bruce had died. His achievements and harsh struggle over the years had taken its toll. The king died at the relatively young age of fifty-four years old. Succeeding in the fight for independence for his country, his last wish was for his heart, once dead, to be carved from his corpse and ceremoniously taken and delivered to the Holy Land. His friend the Earl of Douglas (Black Douglas) took several knights and retainers on this journey and on route in Southern Spain, they ended up aiding Alphonso of Castille in his fight against Muhammad IV Sultan of Granada. The Battle of Teba in August 1330 was about to begin. The brave Douglas took the fight to the Moors. A tactician of countless battles and with a fearless reputation, in this encounter with the foreign enemy he found his knights in the thick of the action but unaided by his Castilian allies. The Moors fell to his initial charge but rallied, and seeing the Scots outnumbered fought on. Douglas was cut down and killed before the Castilians joined the fray and won the battle. One of his captains, Sir Simon Lockhart, oversaw the following victory in which the Moor army was cut to pieces and retreated with great loss of dead and prisoners. One Moor prisoner was ransomed back to his wife, and in exchange, a strange red heart shaped stone was part of the ransom fee along with much silver. Sir Lockhart was told the gemstone had healing properties for cattle if put in the water they drank. This stone remained at the Lockhart family seat in Renfrewshire. For years to come, the stone made its reputation by being lent out for big sums of money to cure cattle. The judges at Isobell's trial asked for the "Lee Stone" (named after Sir Simon Lockhart's family Lee) to take the bewitchment from the cattle.

Isobell Young told the jury that she had the skills to cure the cattle herself without the magical Lee Stone. The method she gave in court probably gave her own lawyer a heart attack! She described her cure as… "killing a cat and an ox and then burying them in a deep hole covered in salt in the infected cattle's field."

The Lee Penny was refused to the court by the owner, but water already treated by the relic was given and administered to the beasts who remarkably recovered back to full health. Isobell's lawyers, Mr Lawrence Magill and David Primrose, took the court floor and delivered in her defence:

> Mr George Sandies Mill stalling, and the fishing drought, was nothing but natural causes and nothing to confirm as Witchcraft!
> The man who lost the use of his limbs and became lame was already many years lame and his ailment could not be put down as Witchcraft!
> "The Devils Mark" found by the Witch Pricker was nothing but an old scar caused by an ulcer.

But this defence, the prosecution lawyer Sir Thomas Hope destroyed by adding,

> What was urged by the prisoner in her defence contradicted what was charged by the public in his indictment.

That was all it took to convince the jury that she was guilty of Witchcraft!

Isobell Young never stood a chance... she was sentenced on the 4th February to be strangled and burnt on Castlehill in Edinburgh.

The old Seagate area of Dundee from an 1800s drawing, where Grissell Jaffray burned in 1669.

CHAPTER 11

THE DUNDEE WITCH GRISSELL JAFFRAY 1669

Sunday 3rd of January 1841, Dundee: David Tanish, a mason in the city, stoked the fires for the coming church service in the South church. It was 6 o'clock, and he had to get the church warm enough for the service, using huge logs to build the fire. But once finished, and with a proud fire burning, he had to do the same duty to the two other churches next door... the three churches that sat right next to each other!

Dundee's three churches before 1841... South, East, and North Church

David Tanish was next door starting the log fires in the other churches when the burning pile of logs in the

South church hearth collapsed. A burning piece of timber rolled towards the window where the flames reached the foot of the tall curtains. The flames travelled upwards to the wooden roof, then it quickly spread to the East church next door. The Dundee Fire service regulars reached the scene and heroically fought the blaze but couldn't stop it reaching the North Church, which the out of control fire also burnt down. All three churches were lost to the fire, but the fire had also consumed the fine library inside holding many rare accounts of the city; records and books of Dundee, some from its established Franciscan Monastery founded as far back as 1280. It was a cruel priceless loss to Dundee's rich history. Presbytery records were all but gone.

In the fire perished the trial records of the Witch Grissell Jaffray. An interesting character and story worthy of inclusion, but what information we do have of her comes from parishes and authors outwith Dundee who wrote about her sad story. What we know of her is pieced together jigsaw style and relayed here…

For a while, she was regarded as nothing but myth as only scant records remained on her. Her story is most unsettling. Only poems and spoken tales continued to keep her story alive, until researchers pulled together what was known of her from other parishes and logged them in "the charter house in Dundee" with the remaining archives.

From the Kirk session register,

> Auchterhouse parish, 22nd April 1669, Minister W.Mason-Ingles writes…
>
> By the order of the Presbytery of Dundee, action was ordered to be taken against all guilty of

> Witchcraft—the Magistrates of Dundee were particularly desired to use all diligence for trying them further, they compelled with the Presbytery instructions and appointed those suspected of Witchcraft to be banished which was done, and the act put to execution.

What we have here is evidence of a trial for Witchcraft in Dundee. No names are mentioned, but the Dundee tolbooth jail reports on 11th November mentions Grissell Jaffray where Henry Scrymsour of St Marys church, John Guthrie of South Church, and William Rait of St Pauls find her Guilty of Witchcraft. That's East, South, and North parishes.

The Register office of Edinburgh gives further evidence twelve days later on the 23rd November and names her again…

> Dundee 23rd November 1669
>
> Anent such are delated for Witchcraft the Ministers having also reported to the council that Grissel Jaffrey—Witch at her execution did delate several persons as being guilty of Witchcraft. To them and therefore desired that for their exoneration some council might be taken against them delated— the Council in order nominated the Provost the present baillies, old Baillies and the Dean of Guild and others to meet with Ministers and commune with them on the said matter, and consider the best ways may be taken with the delated.

On this record, it seems she had already been burned. The register of the Privy Council is given as a source for her burning on November 11, 1669, from the *History of Dundee* book by Mr Thomson in 1874 (p.102), but he may have taken it from the tolbooth records I've just quoted from above, where it states, "she's in the tolbooth on witchcraft charges."

What is known of her is that she may have originated from Aberdeen where there was a big Jaffray family. She did marry a James Butchart, and in surviving Kirk sessions it says he is a Maltman (brewer). One surviving record from the Town Council minutes of Dundee 21st November (ten days after her burning) states that, "James Butchart husband of Grissel Jaffrey (Maltman), desirous to be admitted to the benefit of the hospital recommended by his good fame and reputation of the Minister of the Kirk session."

After a Witch burning, it was law for the husband to foot the bill for his wife's burning. All expenses, from timber and tar barrels to torture and minister's fees to what the executioner drank during the burning, had to be paid for. Records still exist of the bills given to the husbands of the Pittenweem Witches (Weem Witches) in 1645. They were given £40 bills for burning their women as Witches in a day where you got paid a penny a day for working in the farm fields. Is this why he's asking for the benefits of the Church hospital? He's paid out for Grissell's burning and left himself destitute!

A horrible footnote to poor Grissell's story is really what made her case stand out from others. We know naught about why she was charged with Witchcraft or the details of her arrest and confessions due to the records lost in the fire. But what did make her famous was her story carried in a poem made out to her by a long lost author, who from word of mouth of her sad tale, constructed a long telling poem. It's from here Witch Grissell Jaffray's story becomes legend.

The poem covers the sorry tale of her son being at sea for many months, and while trading abroad, finally comes home with his ship full of merchant stock. Coming into the Tay river outlet towards the Dundee city, he sees a commotion at the sea front near "the Seagate building"; a crowd of people and a huge burning pyre. As his boat gets closer, he sees it's a Witch burning. Closer still and he finally recognises the face in the flames… it is none other but his own mum, Grissell Jaffray. So disgusted with the event and with the people of Dundee, he pulled the anchors and set sail again, never to return to the city.

This sorry tale brought my eye to the Grissell Jaffray case; it's only written in poetry, and no official records can confirm the story, but I believe the poem was written based on factual accounts. It does have many chapters and may give long lost details of her accusations in a poet's words. It's a lengthy read, but I have selected the important information in the text for you here.

THE LEGEND OF THE BURNING OF MISTRESS JAMPHRAY

> She has ta'en her long staff in her shaky hand,
> And gaen up the stair of Will Mudie's land,
> She has looked in the face of Will Mudie's wean,
> And the wean it was dead that very same e'en.

Next day she has gane to the Nethergate,
And looked ower the top of Ron Rorisons gate,
Where he and his wife having got into brangles,
Rob's grey mare Bess that night took the strangles.
It was clear when she went to Broughty Ferry,
She sailed in an egg shell in place of a Ferry,
And when she had pass'd by the Tower of Claypotts,
John Fairweather's gelding was seized with the bots,
And his black horse Billy was seized the same even,
Not by the bots but the spanking spavin.
And on she went to Monifieth,
she met an auld man with the wind in his teeth,
Are you the Witch o Bonnie Dundee?
You may ask the wind, and then will see!
And such was the wickedness in her spite,
The man took the toothache that very night.
With John Throw's wife she was at drawing daggers,
And twenty of John Sheep took the staggers.

When Luckie Macrobie's sweet milk wouldn't erne,
the reason was clear—she bewitched the concern.
True! no man could swear that he ever saw,
her flee on a broomstick over North Berwick Law;
Then sure there was something far worse than a frolic,
When half of Dundee was seized by the cholic.
True! Nobody knew that she gaed on the howf,
For dead man's fat to bring home in her loof,
To brew from the mixture of henbane and savin,
for Hell broth for those thirsting for heaven.
Ere good Provost Syme was taken by tremor,

It was known the Provost had called her a limmer;
And when Baillie Nicholson broke his thigh bone,
had she not been seen that day in his home.
When the Ferry boat sank in the crossing the Tay,
She was on the Craig pier the very same day.
She kept in her house an auld pet,
That bird was the Devil, in truth the old pet was daintily treated,
because her black soul was impignorated.

The barrels are brought from Norway,
Well-seasoned with plenty of Norway pitch,
All dried and split for that jubilee day,
The day of the holocaust of a Witch.
The prickers are chosen-hang man and brother,
And fixed were the fees of their work of love,
to prick an old woman who was a mother,
And felt still the yearnings of motherly love,
for she had a son, a noble young fellow,
Who sailed in a ship of his own on the sea,
for a cargo of wine to this Bonnie Dundee.
On the long red sands of old Dundee,
Out at the hem of the ebbing sea,
They have fixed a long pole deep in the sand,
And around it have piled it with defty hand,
The rosined staves of Norway wood,
Four feet high and four feet broad,
To burn, amidst flames of burning pitch,
So rare a chimera lept a Witch.

Ho! Yonder comes from the emptying town,
A crowd of five thousand all rushing down,
deep in the midst of this jubilant throng,
A harmless woman is hurried along.
She is weary and wheezing with lac of breath,
And ower her face is the pallor of death.
They have doffed her clothes till all but stark,
They have tied her with ropes in her cutty sark.
Their lances and glances each long-pronged fork,
As though the wild flames it is quick at work,
The flames lap around her like forked levin;
The priests send up their prayers to heaven.

There's a ship in the Tay on the rising tide,
she has come that day from distant land,
The Captain stands there the helm beside,
A telescope holding in his left hand,
"What is it that's burning there?
They are burning an old woman as a Witch;
And thy woman, she is your mother dear."
Then Captain Jamphray silent stood,
and sad and sorrowful man was he,
he turned the helm in a gloomy mood,
and said "Farewell forever to Bonnie Dundee."

Old engraving of Dundee harbour... where Grissell's son, months at sea brought his boat in towards the harbour where he saw a great crowd and commotion on the beach by the Seagate. As his boat neared the harbour, he saw his own mother, tied to a wooden stake and burning as a Witch.

SOURCES

George Fraser Black, *A calendar of cases of witchcraft in Scotland, 1510–1727* (1938)

The register of the Privy Council of Scotland, Vol.3, 1629 (1901)

Wilson's Tales of the Borders, & of Scotland, Vol 7 (1888)

CHAPTER 12

THE DUNDEE NAKED SCHNECKLE EATERS

My stepdaughter Amber, on the last of her high school days, had amassed enough hard-earned booty in "A" grade Highers to qualify for basically any university of her choice. Proud parents saw her disappear to England and the University of Chichester for the next few years!

With a huge, now empty, bedroom, we decided to foster a wee German girl. Lea was her name. Lea had previously stayed for a year on the barren landscape of Benbecula and over time regaled us with her stories. She mentioned she had a nightmare time getting used to the massive slugs that roam the part of the island where she stayed; she had never seen them so large. Her pronunciation of them was limited, but in German it was a *Nacktsschnecke*, which means Naked Snail!

My partner and I found this hilarious, "a naked snail" (which indeed a slug actually is when you think about it!). So, to us, "slugs", that inhabit my hens' grain bin in massive numbers, have become "Naked Schneckles!" This leads us to our next story, set in Dundee 1645.

At the turn of 1641, a violent strain of smallpox was evident in Scotland. It took the feeble and elderly without mercy. In Aberdeen, records state that ten children a day were being buried. More calamity followed in the following year when the fishing fleets found that the white fish stocks normally in abundance had disappeared from the waters. With heavy rain for months, the crops now gathered were frugal and spoiled. It is against this background of woe that the plague now arose from a ship docking in Leith, Edinburgh, and then spread its cargo of death and misery across the land. With this, now came civil war and the clash of great Highland armies.

Dundee was a walled city, and when General Montrose arrived in April 1645 with his thousands of Highlanders, the Dundee Council forbade them entry. Although many sympathised with the king's cause against Parliament, the thought of feeding men in their thousands just after seeing through a rough winter and emptying what little the city had in its meagre stores, was the main prevention from enabling them access.

Nevertheless, Montrose's Highlanders forced their way into the city, breaking down the northwest wall and gaining entry. Several properties were burnt, and they ransacked the city, killing those who tried to protect their property and emptying the city of anything of value. The great vaults of wine and beer were discovered and handsomely attacked. By nightfall, every kilted Highland warrior was drunk out their mind, and it's no mean miracle that their enemies were discovered no more than a mile from the gates of Dundee at dawn... and every Highlander escaped out the city northwards with Montrose, hangovers and all, escaping before they were confronted by the new army.

The Highlanders moved on as the other army arrived from the West, leaving a barren and very threadbare Dundee.

As hunger and pestilence now reigned, the population of Dundee struggled for survival. Horses and dogs were slaughtered for meat by the utterly desperate people, turned now to an existence with nothing left in the stores, not even seed for replanting crops.

As the peasants buried the dead in the Dundee hills and fields, whispers started on the question of two young girls, who had, in their wisdom when the Highland Army arrived and broke in the city gates and to avoid molestation and the pestilence raging in the city, taken their belongings into a small abode near "Bonnetmakers Hill"[13] Nothing was significantly unusual in what they did or where they stayed. The law in Scotland at this time forbid a woman to live in a property on her own, but the two girls held their own company close, and to jealous eyes, the two girls were a picture of great health and vitality compared with the locals from the city.

But a leader arose to gather a mob, and with violent intent they marched to the girls' bothy to face them with charges that they could only be untouched by pestilence and starvation because they were protected by Witchcraft!

At the last moment before being dragged to trial, the girls relented to questions of their health and wellbeing and showed the secret of their sustenance. To their own embarrassment and shame, it wasn't devilish intervention, but a certain hellish scene did show itself... a barrel in the

---

13. Bonnetmakers Hill was outwith the town walls and so a free trade area exempt from taxes but also at the mercy of vagabonds and villainy, and, as they had found out, also marauding armies. It also had the distinction of being known as "Rotten Row", a terminology reflecting the plague and possibly where the dead were buried or where the pestilence had struck before. Today it is known as "Hilltown" situated north of the city and south of the main road.

corner of the house was revealed to be filled very generously with giant grey slugs! Or Latin name "Limacina", or a bucketful of "Naked Schneckles"!

The girls had found them very plentiful, finding them in the grasses of the hills around them. Boiled with a touch of salt, it may horrify the reader, but it had kept the girls alive and healthy. Their proper *Gordon Ramsey's Kitchen Nightmare* was accepted by the rabble and even applauded for their ingenuity. The girls were then left in peace.

I found to my horror that today several recipes exist for a slug meal! The English Chef and television presenter Hugh Fearnley Whittingstall has the honour of constructing a dish for the slimy horrors.

I will leave the reader to find that themselves. But as I write in Oct 2019, and the Brexit debate goes on and on, predictions of a "Mad Max" future after Brexit with food shortages and riots at empty shelves in the shops resurface… I may have to keep an eye on my "Naked Schneckles" in the hen-bin!… Hmmmmm yummy!

Hmmmmm lovely

SOURCES

William Wallace Fyfe, *Summer life on land and water (at South Queensferry)* (1851)

Robert Chambers, *Domestic Annals of Scotland* (1859–61)

Photo credit: model: Callum Low (the coward wouldn't eat one for a tenner!)

CHAPTER 13

EDINBURGH, 1670
THE MADNESS OF MAJOR WEIR

The West Bow area of Edinburgh, a steep street with Mr Weir's house centre right.

Edinburgh, 1670: He sat in church as usual; his dress and looks were of what a gentleman should wear. He once held the rank as a Major in the city guard and lived in the West Bow area, his house halfway up a steep hill that his 70-year-old frame now struggled to walk. His wife Isobel had died a while back, and he shared his house with his sister Jean who brought money into the house with a spinning business.

He had a gracefulness about him and could converse

with great knowledge. For all that saw and knew him in church, he was noted as having a wonderful fluency in extemporary prayers.

But today was different, there was a conscience like a cancer eating him up inside, something was awakening in this man's old age... secrets... dirty secrets! He thought the Devil had held his thoughts too long. With his body succumbing to the pains of age, he dwelt on how many years he had left in him, and he felt he must confess his wicked dealings and what his remarkable guilt had hidden in the shadows too long now.

Walking from the church, he passed an open cellar where people were drinking and doing business. It was no crime to share a drink with friends, but this proprietor looked to Mr Weir, knowing him to be an acquaintance, and gave him a welcoming gesture. But the man's name was Mr Burne, and at sight of him, Mr Weir's conscience flamed again like a wicked portent of days to come. He fell into fits, foaming at the mouth and shouting out the word... "BURN, BURN, BURN!"

He retired home reflecting on his Bible teachings of how flames were prepared for the damned at the final reckoning. His seventy years of secrets... dirty secrets of where for a great sinner, when the curtains of death fold, the soul would be judged on the life the person had led... in Mr Weir's opinion he was in for a hot time of it! The gates of hell were beckoning his soul to step in...

The canker of madness was eating the mind of Mr Weir. His guilt absolute, and it now so haunted his soul, he terrified himself to walk over running water as Witches were supposed to fear the cleanliness of the Lord's baptism water and the purity that came from it. Purity cannot mix with the filth of a soul delivered to the Devil.

The word "burn" still pricked his conscience; the Devil was mocking him. He solemnly took his tortured mind to his friend Lord Abbot Hall, then Provost of Edinburgh, who listened as the Major confessed all. He exclaimed all his secrets whilst held in his erratic terror…

The Lord Abbot would listen, then exclaim: "He was horrified that nature was capable of such crimes as Mr Weir had just told him."

Mr Weir said the Devil had lulled him into a deep security, and he must confess his wickedness and remarkable guilt. He confessed to…

> Defiling his sister since she was 10, having carnal dealings with her ever since, committed incest with his own daughter Jane, he had many crimes of fornication with his own servant Bessie Weems for 20 years, he had lain with cattle even horses and even lain with the Devil himself and three other species of animal.

In a day where sex outside wedlock was seen as a criminal offence (once a capital offence from Mary Queen of Scots' Parliament of 1563), the above confession was enough for a dozen heart attacks at once to the Lord Abbot! Major Weir and his sister were arrested, and in her own confession, the words of an old confused bewildered man were backed up with solid evidence. She agreed with her brother's statement and even added more grizzly, perverted details. Margaret Weir said…

> Her brother and sister (daughter) had all lain together in a barn at Wicket Shaw, and all were naked together, the bed did shake. They had travelled with the Devil in a horse drawn carriage to Musselburgh and back, Mr Weir had lain with the Devil and he looked like a beautiful woman.

Now rumourmongers went wild on outlandish stories about the Weirs: he had a walking stick that was the power of his evil, Jane could spin wool three times faster than anyone else because of demonic help, and both had spirit familiars that did their evil work.

What is remarkable about this case is that everything was casually confessed: no torture or pre-written statements to sign. It was as if both had a lot on their shoulders that they wanted to get off; as if once confessed it was a massive relief to them. Both were looked at by doctors from Edinburgh and declared sane—the statements would hold as evidence! In the Edinburgh Tolbooth, Mr Weir asked for no mercy but cried out remorselessly in the darkness of his cell. Ministers and jailers said, "he did lay under a violent apprehension of the heavy wrath of God."

The Dean of Edinburgh came to confess him in the tolbooth, and the old Major cried to him…

> Torment me no more before my time as I am tormented enough already. Trouble me no more with your beseeching of me to repent, for I know my

> sentence of damnation is already sealed and if your soul was my soul instead you would find your exhortations impertinent and troublesome for, I find nothing within me but blackness and darkness, brimstone and burning for me at the bottom pits of hell.

He and his sister were brought to trial on the 6th of April 1670. Mr William Murray and John Prestoune Advocates (made judges by commission) sat and read the charges to the pair...

> Item 1... That Mr Weir defiled his sister since she was 10, and had carnal dealings with her ever since.
> Item 2... committed incest with his own daughter, Mary Bourman, his dead wife's daughter.
> Item 3... Bestiality with a mare and a cow.

Mr Thomas Weir had been a highly respected Presbyterian figure, a man who had seen Military action in 1641 suppressing Irish Papists. He had been born and brought up in Lanarkshire, joining the army there and distinguishing himself until he took the rank of Major. In his old age, he commanded part of the Town Guard in Edinburgh. In this position, he had looked after General Montrose who had been captured after his failed rebellion supporting Charles 1st. Mr Weir was his personal guard and jailer. He took great efforts to taunt his prisoner, not having much love for Papist sympathisers. His honourable background kept the charges of Witchcraft away from his own charge sheet. But it could not protect his sister. He was unanimously found guilty and sentenced to be strangled at the stake and his body to burned to ashes on the 11th April.

Jane Weir was next in the dock and accused of Witchcraft and incest, and also consulting with Witches when she lived in Dalkeith (this could be 1661, when a massive trial in Dalkeith involved ten witches). She confessed that her own mother had been a Witch, and she had learned all from her.[14] She was sentenced to hang for her crimes on the 12th of April.

Mr Weir was strangled and burned on the 11th. A newspaper covering the case came out in 1688 called the *Ravillac redivivus*, sharing its pages with the Trial of James Mitchel, a covenanter recently killed. It gives intimate details of Mr Weir's time in jail repenting, and of his burning where witnesses insisted, "His body gave manifest tokens of its impurity as soon as it started to burn, no sooner was he burnt to ashes when bystanders who knew him said the burnt figure in the flames was not the form of Mr Weir." His sister's execution was another spectacle for the bystanders… on the ladder to her hanging, she tried to take off all her clothes to the watching crowd. The hangman tried to intervene, when the 70-year-old brutally slapped him. His response was to push her off the ladder ungainly

---

14. I find in my records 1629, April 15, Lanarkshire (where the Weirs were born and raised) a Janet Weir was one of sixteen apprehended and interrogated for "crymes of witchcraft, using of charmes and enchantments and other devilish practices." Most were convicted and burnt… This Janet Weir may have been their mother the Witch Jane Weir mentions in her confession.

where she strangled to death slowly, dangling on the rope naked.

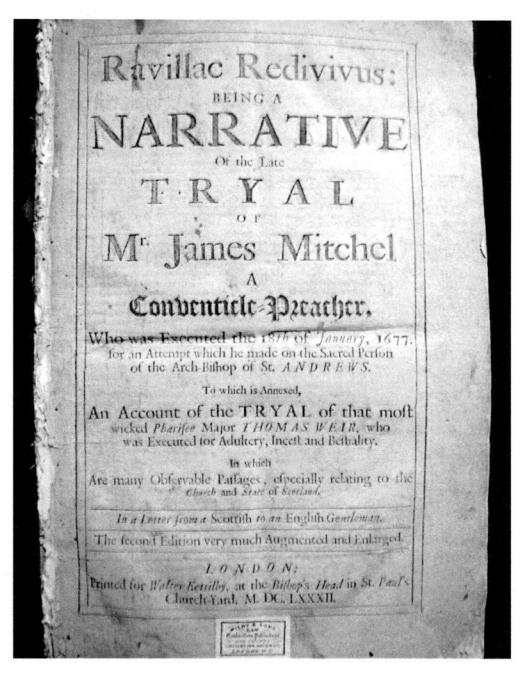

Author's copy of the *Ravillac redivivus*, giving all the horrid details of the trial.

An amazing case: I find it very similar to the American sexual pervert, old Albert Fish born in 1870, two hundred years after Thomas Weir's death. Although Fish would go down for murder and cannibalism, his crime sheet was much longer in perversions. Albert Fish was caught as Weir was, in old age, with two-dozen needles inserted into his groin for sexual satisfaction. He confessed freely to horrendous perversions, as did Weir, and was executed on the electric chair in the USA, where he was quite excited about the prospects of the chair as he hadn't tried that before!

Recently a researcher intrigued by Major Weir's story went to the West Bow area of Edinburgh, and armed with ink engravings from the 1700s, he could still identify the location of Mr Weir's house.

Mr Weir's house today, black door to the right opens to the stone stairs to the original house.

Sources

Robert Chambers, *Traditions of Edinburgh* revised edition (1868)

George Hickes, *Ravillac redivivus, a narrative of the late tryal of mr. James Mitchel who was executed the 18th of January last, for an attempt which he made on the sacred person of the Archbishop of St. Andrews. To which is annexed, An account of the tryal of Thomas Weir. In a letter from a Scottish to an English gentleman [really by G. Hickes.]* (1678)

The register of the Privy Council of Scotland, Vol.3, 1629– (1901)

CHAPTER 14

THE FORFAR WITCHES, 1661

This item has several names in the records... Scold's bridle/ Witch's branks... The Forfar Witches were pulled through the town and burnt wearing them! The item was fetched from the ashes and used on the next Witch to burn... this one in the author's collection.

The following trial follows the usual scaremongering and build-up of fear in a Witch case till it reaches unbelievable proportions of utter nonsense. But by this time, everything had been recorded as evidence, and as each Witch gets interviewed and tortured further, the story takes greater strides from each Witch to outdo the previous Witch's confession with more outrageous tales, twisting the story into an incredible jumble of lies.

The Witch torturer here was a very experienced man, a man of lies and deceit. Being paid a huge £6 for every Witch he could confess,[15] he manipulated the Forfar accused in tortures and fear to obtain whatever he wanted from them in their confessions.

Helen Guthrie, the wife of James Howat living in Forfar, was arrested on charges of Witchcraft. In the tolbooth jail, she confessed to having three strange, weathered pages of paper, each with drops of blood on them. The pages helped her find and identify other Witches, and with this she could successfully confirm the person was a Witch within twenty-four hours in their company. The skills she admitted to have, she said had been given to her from a nearby Witch called Janet Galloway in the village of Kirriemuir.[16] Helen, in the trial notes, is stated as being, "a very drunken woman, living a very wicked life, a terrible curser and would give a terrible opinion to any person." She claimed to know who a Witch was even if they were not present.

This frightened the baillies of Forfar. The minister, Mr Alex Robertsone, requested a Witch Pricker to extract what information was needed on the threat of more Witches in his community. Enter the Tranent-based Witch Pricker, Mr John Kincaid and his apprentice David Cowan.

---

15. 85 days wages in 1660, Scots pound 1/13 of English pound.
16. A Witch was found and burned in 1662 Kirriemuir called Janet Walker, this may be the same woman under her husband's name.

Mr Kincaid set to work torturing Helen Guthrie. Within a day, he had further Witch names and the people they had cast their spells on. The new accused were:

- Elspet Alexander who had cast a spell on David Dickson,
- Helen Alexander who had cast a spell on David Walker,
- Janet Stow who had cast a spell on John Coupar,
- John Tailzour who had cast a spell on Andrew Watsone,
- Kathrin Portour who had cast a spell on James Persone and George Sutie.

With another six Witches committed to the tolbooth, Helen Guthrie still hadn't finished confessing. She put the Kirk in a panic as she now openly confessed, with more help from the torturer, that she was a murderer: "When the bridge over St Johnstone was carried away in the storm, she murdered her half sister Margaret Hutchen at the age of six or seven." She confessed that she,

> had been at Devil's meetings several times with her own mother, the Devil in the shape of an Iron hewed man, at the meeting was the following Witches dancing... Catherine Porter... Mary Rynd... Issobell Syrie... Andrew Watsone... Janet Stout... Christian Stout... Christian Whyt... Andrew Watsone... John Tailzior... and George Elies.

As we can see from the above names, now victims of Witchcraft became accused themselves... Andrew Watsone being one. The others were now squeezed into the confines of the Forfar tolbooth. As were John Bonny and Alexander Heich who, "made merry with the Devil."

The daughter of Helen Guthrie was brought forward at John Kincaid's request and pricked. She now confessed to,

> drinking and dancing with the Devil at the Loch at Forfar, he presented himself all dressed in black, and he renamed her "the pretty dancer". Kisses were shared, God was renounced, and sex was had with her mother!

Elspet Allexander, spouse to John Moffat, now confessed she was guilty of Witchcraft, and after Kincaid had finished with her, he found the Devil's mark on her shoulder. She declared she was "ready to suffer death for it." The Devil had baptised and renamed his coven; the new names were:

- Elspet Alexander... now called Alison,
- Issobell Syrie... now called Horse,
- Helen Guthrie... now called Whyt Witch,
- Jonet Wowit... now called pretty dancer,
- Mary Rynd... Now called the Devils date,
- John Tailzior... now called Belzebub.

More torture and prickings brought further confessions...

Jonet Stout confessed herself guilty and willing to suffer death for it; she identified all the names already accused... was told by the Devil she would never want for anything!

Catherine Porter confessed "to be a very Wicked woman, almost blind but she could see the Devil." She was a terrible curser. She admitted during the trial to meeting the Devil at the bleaching green with two other Witches who had already been executed.

Issobell Syrie confessed to be a Witch and would take the guilt with it. She had sex with the Devil at many meetings. Admitted to killing baillie Wood by a spell. Made him drink a potion of crushed toad heads with a piece of a dead man's skull... he died 20 days later. All this was obtained without torture. But all she needed was to see the Witches already processed and the bloody mess the Witch Pricker Kincaid had left of them. No wonder she confessed so easily.

John Tailzour confessed he met the Devil several times and was lent money by him. The Devil had a brown horse when he appeared to him at Petterden.

Agnes Spark went to secret dances with Issobell Syrie at a place called little Miln, where a dozen other Witches danced, she had sex with the Devil.

More confessions came from Helen Guthrie, even worse and more damming than her previous confession of murdering her stepsister... At the parish church wall by the south wall, Andrew Watsoun had with him an infant child no more than a baby. An unbaptised one when the Witches killed it, ripped it to pieces, and made pies out of the feet, hands, and part of the head and buttocks. All the Witches ate the pie, and it would give protection against them ever confessing... it would make them immune to torture.

Issobell Smith confessed adultery 20 years ago, a

covenant with the Devil, and renounced God. The Devil did promise her three half pennies a year, and he was a nice gentleman. At several meetings, she saw "a whole army of Witches!" She then admitted to killing James Grey with a spell by blowing dust in his face during an argument over a cow's pasture.

With so much horrifying evidence of murder and cannibalism, the judges of 45 persons ordained a verdict of guilty of Witchcraft on: Issobell Smith... Helen Guthrie... Issobell Syrie... Helen Cothall... John Tailzour... Catherin Porter... Elspet Alexander... Jonet Stout.

All were to burn individually. It's recorded they were led to the stake wearing a Witch's branks and burned with it. The iron branks would be recovered from the dying ashes to be fixed on the next Witch for burning!

The others accused were whipped and banished from the town. The baillies, so happy with the thorough cleansing of the town of Forfar, decided to reward the Witch Pricker with the honour of "the freedom of the borough," a burgess-ship reward to him and David Cowan his apprentice.

The Witch Pricker Kincaid and his apprentice David Cowan, full of riches and the plaudits from his employers from Forfar Council, left for Edinburgh and immediately identified another Witch. Without receiving a commission or permission, they set about pricking her. Full of their Forfar endorsements and a belief in their righteousness, they thought themselves a law above others. But they were soon stopped by the Edinburgh Sherriff and arrested. Slung in the tolbooth where many of his victims ended up, Kincaid cried in despair and used his frailty and age (about

60) to get the prison officers to relent and release him on bail. He never interrogated another Witch and died in obscurity in Tranent. His apprentice David Cowan carried on the trade, and he himself was arrested as a fraud in 1678.

SOURCES

George Fraser Black, *A calendar of cases of witchcraft in Scotland, 1510–1727* (1938)

G. R. Kinloch, *Reliquiæ Antiquæ Scoticæ, illustrative of Civil and Ecclesiastical Affairs. From original manuscripts* (1848)

Alan Reid, *The Regality of Kirriemuir* (1909)

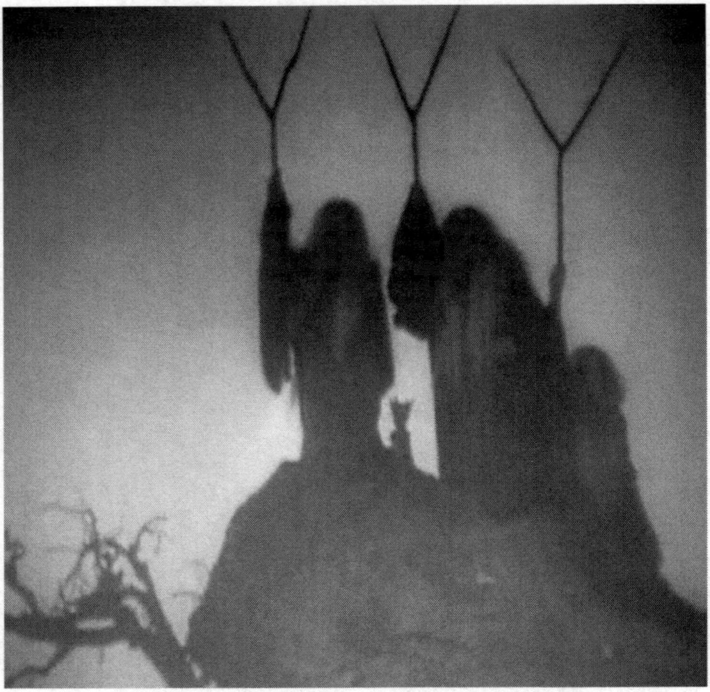

CHAPTER 15

THE FORRES WITCHES
THE REAL WITCHES OF MACBETH

Scotland 1040: the threat of war was once again over the Northern lands. Duncan was King of Scotland, and the Norsemen under Thorfinn had risen. The Norse lords' Black Raven Banners struck fear as the Viking hordes spread out from the castle stronghold of Torfness near Elgin in Moray, where Burghead Castle was Thorfinn's headquarters. The castle (Broch) had timber ramparts 20 foot high and a masonry wall facing the sea equally as large. Inside was a Viking town protected handsomely by the wall and full of battle-hardened warriors.

    King Duncan's attack was in two prongs: from the sea and the land. His sea galleys were no match for the Viking maritime war machine, and off the coast of Caithness they met and were worsted by the Dragon-headed fleet of Thorfinn. On land, King Duncan's force vastly outnumbered Thorfinn's Vikings, but valour beats odds every time. Duncan's army contained a regiment of Irish mercenaries, and they were first to test the Viking steel. They fought bravely but were no match and were quickly routed off the field. Duncan brought his standard up front to face Thorfinn's men head on, and the might of his army and steel went with him. Thorfinn was the target to bring this battle to a quick end, and he could be seen fighting in his golden helmet and coat of mail, his long sword flashing in the sunlight, slaying foes and leading by example. He spurred on his men to defeat King Duncan's army and send the king running from the field of slaughter.

The king ran with the remains of his army and one of his lieutenants, "Macbeth". As they ran eastwards, they neared Bothgounan (now called Pitgaveny) near the head of Loch Spynie, and here Macbeth turned on his master and cut him down and killed him. With King Duncan dead, Macbeth took the Scottish throne and formed a treaty with Thorfinn, and hostilities ceased between the Scots and Vikings. In reality, Thorfinn's men were the victors on sea and land, but he had lost so many men, Macbeth, if he wished, could summon up more armies and finish of Thorfinn; so, an uneasy peace was created that suited both parties.

What made Macbeth turn on his master has been romanticised by William Shakespeare in his play *Macbeth*; meeting three Witches on the moors of Forres, where they prophesised he would be crowned king. Written in 1606 to great acclaim from the new British Monarch James 1st, we know where he got his source material for his character Macbeth. But what about the three Witches of Forres heath? Well, we have to go back to Forres in Caithness, Northern Scotland, in 961 AD and find yet another Scottish king who was at war with the Vikings.

King Duff (or Duffus) was King of Scots from 962 to 967 AD and had already lost his father, King Indulf, to the Viking invaders four years previously. With trouble brewing again, he suddenly took ill after going through the lands of Forres to Scone where he finally rested. He demanded a search for Witches as he was convinced that at Forres he had been bewitched.

Three women were soon found at Forres, and it's claimed they had been playing with a doll made from wax and were melting it into the fire — a waxen image of the king! The Witches were taken without trial and led still alive to the top of a local hill in Forres called Cluny Hill, where three empty herring barrels were sitting waiting for them. The three women were confused to the purpose of the barrels.

I'm rather hardened to the process of torture in the Witch trials. With the many documents at my disposal, I have read horror stories of women and men being abused in heartless methods as parish courts tried all they could to extract confessions. The nature and repugnant manners of ministers using the name of God to justify their actions was always recorded in the records. It's hard at times to realise you're not reading fiction. I have extracts from the courts where victims accused of Witchcraft have skin ripped off and vinegar poured on them; beaten and brutalised people managing a cross as a signature to signify a confession as their fingers are all broken by the tortures put to them. Man was inventive in the Witch hunts at coming up with many industrious methods of hurting his fellow man. The *Malleus Maleficarum* only scratches the surface of horrid ideas to extract confessions. What came next at Cluny Hill, Forres, tops the lot for its ingenuity in pain.

As the crowd waited at the bottom of the hill, the authorities placed the women in each of the three barrels, then fixed the wooden lids on them. They then hammered huge iron nails into the side of the barrels, piercing through the wood to stick through with inches to spare, the woman still trapped inside, unaware to what was in store for them. They turned the barrels on their sides and then rolled them one by one down the hill… the Witch trapped inside with all the nails stuck through the side would be reduced to nothing but mince by the time the barrel stopped rolling. Here they covered the barrel in timber and heather and burnt it to ashes at the very spot where it stopped rolling.

Three boulders were left on the spot to commemorate the last resting place and where the women had all burned. They were still standing until the early 1800s, when the local estate owner decided to smash them up and use them in the masonry of nearby buildings. One was saved before it was destroyed and remains today with a small plaque to commemorate the three Witches.

William Shakespeare was in Aberdeen in 1601 as a guest of King James I in October of that year. He either visited the moor himself, or the stories in the local taverns fuelled his thirst for Witchcraft as recently they had a spate of trials (38 between 1596–97, killing around 40).

The author was here recently and viewed the stones. The big stone had been bashed by stone masons eager to add it to the nearby infrastructure. Historians have saved it and fixed it back in place with an iron band. They added the plaque later. It's no mistake that Shakespeare must have heard this tale, and it influenced his play to give him thoughts towards the three Witches he placed on Forres Heath to taunt Macbeth.

For an age the stones were known as "The Three

Sisters", until the 1800s, where we had the destruction of one of the stones. The second stone sits in a corner of a garden on the opposite side of the road. There is still a large hole where the third stone has gone missing... I suspect it sits proudly in someone's garden with the owners unaware to its significance.

The nearby Cluny Hill,

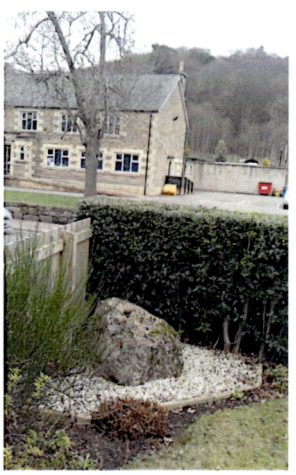

where the poor Witches were launched to their doom, is about one hundred feet high. Its full of wild undergrowth and trees, fully three hundred yards distance from the stones to the top of Cluny Hill. But without the undergrowth, three barrels with their unfortunate contents, if rolled from the top of Cluny Hill, could easily make the position of today's stones, where the mangled contents were burnt where they stopped!

The three Forres Witches from 965 don't appear in official records, their names don't exist, but they do exist in folklore and fleeting history.

The stone sits right on the roadside of Forres near the Police Station on Victoria road. It was famed in a local book in 1932 (*The Pageant of Morayland* by J.B. Richie) but is also written about in *TheGazeteer of Scotland*, 1844.

The Annals of Ulster (431–1540), a book written by monks, gives credence to the Viking movements, and the Irish mercenaries claim King Duffus was killed by his own Scots in 967. His body was hidden under the bridge at Kinloss where it's reported, "the Sun never shone till the body was buried." What we have here (with a bit of research) is information as to a solar eclipse that astronomers today can precisely identify happening on the 10th of July 967! This lends credence to the story of Duffus being murdered and hidden around this time of the eclipse. With the Witch information related to the threat on his life, it's fair to say the information carried in this book is fairly accurate. The three stones sat for near eight hundred years with the history about them being told by word of mouth, till the 1800s when authors started to write about it. Modern historians cannot verify the account without proper records, so it slips into myth.

This would not be the last of Witches found in the area of Forres. The village of Forres would experience Witch hunts in 1663, where in the *Diary of Alexander Brodie* it mentions "1st of May, this day appointed for the trial of the Witches Isobel Elder and Isobel Simpson who would be burned at Forres and died obstinate."

Another Witch was found about this time called Dorothy Calder. She was known as a "kindly canny (clever) Wife" and lived in a house where the suspension bridge now stands. She put the fear of death into a fisherman after he had a great catch of salmon. He boasted of catching a massive fish but kissed it and placed it back in the water as he had caught enough already. Dorothy claimed he had kissed the Devil and his presence was about her. Within 24 hours of this, she was charged with Witchcraft and burnt on the moor at Drumduan. She was tied to a stake and destroyed amid the shouts of a merciless mob! Again, no official files exist of this mob action, or proper date, but its imprint on local folklore keeps it alive and repeated again here for another generation to keep the awful story alive.

Sources

George Fraser Black, *A calendar of cases of witchcraft in Scotland, 1510–1727* (1938)

Alexander Brodie, *The Diary of Alexander Brodie of Brodie 1652–1680...* Spaulding Club (1863)

Robert Chambers, William Chambers, *The Gazetteer of Scotland* (1844)

Martin Coventry, *Castles of Scotland* (2005)

William Maunsell, *Annals of Ulster 431–1540* (1887)

James R. Ritchie, *The Pageant of Morayland* (1932)

Gavin Turreff, *Antiquarian gleanings from Aberdeenshire records* (1859)

CHAPTER 16

IRVINE AND ITS GENTLE TORTURE

Irvine Parish Church late 1700s

The picturesque view of Irvine from a late 1800 engraving shows the 9th century church in its third rebuild. This church was last redesigned in 1774, but as yet I can find no drawing of its form in 1618 when it was used as a prison for Witches. What the 1618 version did have, according to Sir Walter Scott's account in his *Demonology and Witchcraft* (1830), was a high enclosed room in the tower belfry from where one Witch managed to make her escape.

Irvine on the West Coast of Scotland had two Witch hunts, the first one we recall in detail here, where a quarrel between two brothers' wives would lead to the full powers of the Witchcraft trials being instigated. This happened simply on the evidence of a grumpy child who was promised (and never got) a pair of new shoes for her silence! The trial is quite detailed, and for the first time in the thousands of Witch trials I've looked through, the interrogation procedure is ingeniously referred to by the sitting magistrate as "the gentle torture".

Archibald and John Dein were both hard-working men from a decent family. Archibald was a trader in Irvine, while his brother John was the skipper of a cargo boat called "The Gift of God". The boat was owned by the local Provost Andrew Tran and was laden with cargo due for French ports. The voyage could make all involved very rich, and other local lairds had become involved through investing in the venture.

In the background, as this venture was being equipped, John Dein's wife Janet Lyal fell out with Archibald's wife, declaring Margaret Barclay "a thief". Margaret Barclay took the accusation to the doors of the local parish court where on hearing the dispute, they ordered the warring women to shake hands and forget the whole matter. They grudgingly did so in front of the Sunday service, but Margaret was still secretly aggrieved, and with malice in mind, she approached a man well known as an entertainer in the town called John Stewart. His talent was juggling, but Margaret misunderstood his talent and skills, thinking he must have some supernatural deity helping him!

The boat (described as a Bark) went to sea laden with goods, but after a month, there was still no sign of "The Gift of God" returning. A foolish comment to John Dein's worried wife Janet Lyal by the juggler John Stewart was made where he foresaw the boat had gone under to the watery depths and her husband drowned!

The juggler's prediction was proved true when two seamen came to Irvine harbour from an English boat, and the news they brought was grim! They were the only survivors from "The Gift of God". It had hit rocks off Cornwall near Padstow and had been smashed on the shore with the loss of all cargo and crew. Janet's husband John Dein was drowned along with the boat's owner Andrew Tran.

Janet Lyal now made the juggler's words of doom haunt him; she called the church and instigated his prediction to them as an act of premeditated Witchcraft. John Stewart was now juggling for his life as the town baillies, who were friends and fellow boat owners of the of the drowned Andrew Tran and John Dein, set the charges to him of Witchcraft.

During John Stewart's torture process, the parish minister remembered the argument between Margaret Barclay and her sister-in-law Janet Lyal. Before long, John Stewart confessed that he was in the Devil's service and Margaret had come to him asking to be taught the black arts in revenge of her sister-in-law. He had come to Margaret Barclay's house where she and two other women were making a clay figure of a man. They also constructed a clay boat with which they went to the harbour, put it in the water, and cried "mak yer bed among the crabs!" Immediately a huge storm broke out. That was the reason for the Bark sinking… sunk by Witchcraft!

Just as I write this tale a Bark style ship is sitting off the coast from me in Fife.

At her house, said John Stewart, "they entertained the Devil in the figure of a black dog." All this information was taken as he was brutally tortured. A written statement would be sitting for the juggler to sign; when he agreed to sign it... the torture would stop. If not, the process could continue for days until the man was completely broken down by exhaustion and pain.

Margaret Barclay and Isobel Insh were next arrested, both declaring they had never associated with John Stewart. But then appeared Isobel Insh's lovely 8-year-old daughter who was employed as a child minder for Margaret Barclay. Margaret Tailzeor was the child's name, and she declared to the Magistrates she had seen all three persons: John Stewart, Margaret Barclay, and her own mum, Isobel Inch, making the clay idol and ship... she also saw another

14-year-old girl, Issobell Crawford. In the huff, she said: "I was promised a new pair of shoes for my silence, and never got them." This declaration was repeated with her own mum sitting in the court dock. Little Margaret Tailzeor wouldn't change her story even with the desperate expressions of her mother. Margaret never got her shoes as promised and was quite content to give information on the night where the Devil visited in the shape of a black dog, with each word spoken sending her mother Isobel Inch a step closer to the church steeple jail where the torturers were waiting.

Isobel Insh had her feet put in iron restraints, then the torturers had their way with her. That night she tried to escape out a window from the tall steeple while still attached to the restraints. More desperation than thought went into this venture as she fell heavily to the ground several metres below, hurting herself internally.

Isobel made it to court next day in a terrible state, she answered everything but declared her absolute innocence to the accusations. She would die 5 days later from her internal injuries suffered in the fall. In the tolbooth jail, the juggler John Stewart had managed to pull a length of string from his own hat and had fixed it to his cell door. He had fixed the rope around his neck, and holding his knees, leaped head first towards the floor and hanged himself. He was found still alive by the guards but later died.

Margaret Barclay and 14-year-old Issobell Crawford were next in the tolbooth torture room. They placed Margaret in foot stocks, sitting on the floor with both her feet out, then the torturer placed heavy iron bars across her shins. The weight became more painful as they added more metal bars. Up to 30 stone in weight was placed on Margaret's legs before she cried out "tak aff, tak aff!" They removed the weights, whereupon she again denied all her confessions. So, the weights were added again, and it was repeated until she confessed all.

Margaret was upset that the 14-year-old Isobel Crawford was involved and pleaded for "no harm to come to her", but she had named her in her tortures as present at the clay idol making. The confession was there in writing, and with the evidence from John Stewart and the 8-year-old servant girl Margaret Tailzeor, both women were doomed… Both Margaret Barclay and Issobell Crawford were condemned by the local magistrate, the 7th Earl of Eglington, Hugh Montgomerie, where he sentenced them both to burn as Witches. They were burned outside the burgh boundary at Mill Road corner.

In March 1650, another trial for Witchcraft involving twelve Witches is reported in Irvine. In one report it's claimed all twelve were executed in this month.

In April of that year, the Presbytery stated, "finding the sin of Witchcraft growing daily with the works of darkness," and Margaret Cooper, Janet Robinson, and Catherine Montgomerie, "who have all confessed to renounce their baptisms." (could this Catherine Montgomerie be a relation to the 1618 judge, Hugh Montgomerie?)

On May 7th records state, "there is to be an execution

of four persons upon Saturday for the sin of Witchcraft." It looks like another Witch was added to the April catch.

Overall, the 1618 story in Irvine is a sorry tale of bickering between two sisters-in-law connected to a sea tragedy. And a child that never got her new shoes... but what consequences.

A rare photo of the tolbooth building which was demolished in 1862

Sources

George Fraser Black, *A calendar of cases of witchcraft in Scotland, 1510–1727* (1938)

Sir Walter Scott, *Demonology and Witchcraft* (1830)

New stastistical account of Ayrshire p.632

History of Ayr and Wigton Vol 3 p.263

CHAPTER 17

JEAN MAXWELL OF KIRKCUDBRIGHT 28TH JUNE 1805

The George II Witchcraft Repeal Act in 1736 put an end to the ferocious Witch hunts. Access to the death penalty and use of torture was now removed from the hands of the Kirk. The new 1736 Bill still had much milder deterrents... they were worded as...

> No person pretends to exercise or use any kind of Witchcraft or conjuration or undertake to tell fortunes or pretend from his or her skill or knowledge in occult or craft or science to discover where or in what manner any goods or chattels supposed to be lost may be found—every person so offering being thereof lawfully convicted on indictments of information. In that part of Great Britain shall for every such offence suffer imprisonment for the space of one full year. Without bail or mainprize and once every quarter of said year to stand openly in the marketplace pillory for space of one hour and be obliged to give surety for their good behaviour in such time as the court should judge proper.

That we have evidence of late Kirk sessions that still report Witchcraft in Scotland long after the date of 1736 is not unremarkable. In the Parish of Kenmore, we have Margaret Robertson at the Kirk session in June 1747 bitterly complaining that she has been unfairly charged with using Witchcraft and enchantments. Again, in the same parish in 1753, Witchcraft charges were thrown at Donald Thomson's servant Janet McNichol for behaving peculiarly over a stream of south running water. As late as 1805, we have a trial in Kirkcudbright in Galloway, that had it been one hundred years earlier the poor wretch of a girl would have burned as a Witch with all the hatred of the parish courts.

Jean Maxwell was prisoner in the tolbooth of Kirkcudbright. Indicted by the Procurator Fiscal Robert Gordon. Her charges were that:

> the said Jean Maxwell, did upon Thursday 27th, Friday 28th, and Saturday 29th of December last in the year 1805 at little Cocklit in the Parish of Urr pretend to tell fortunes by teacups and the grounds of tea to Jean Davidson servant to Frances Scott farmer in Little Cocklit. And tell her she would bear a bastard to a certain young man called Hugh Rafferton which you said you could prevent by certain means. Causing Jean Davidson to rub or anoint her forehead and other parts of her head from a liquid in a bottle presented by you. So intoxicated and disordered the girl would have done anything you had asked. You seeing the situation declared to her "the Devil would appear and tear her to pieces unless she obeyed your instructions" A Guinea note was produced in which you pricked with nine pins and made her cast it into a fire. You then ordered Jean Davidson to bring a shirt and three shillings for

> you. The shirt was to be thrown into the fire for the Devil to wear.

This bullying and bribery continued with big shoulders of mutton stolen from her master's kitchen and more shillings and another Guinea note. Jean then demanded Jean Davidson marry the man, Hugh Rafferton. More silly demands came when Jean couldn't use a money note already given. It was so new that it could arouse suspicion as to how she had procured it. So, she demanded another shabbier used note—a "tattered note!"—and three shillings more. This was followed the next week with three more demands for meat and more money to keep the Devil at bay.

This was too much; the girl was nothing short of terrified between two evils—getting caught stealing from her master's pantry and wallet, and the thought of the Devil being unhappy with her in not producing his presents.

The servant broke down in front of her employer and then told him everything. Poor simple Jean Davidson was terrified the Devil was going to come for her as she had stopped providing more of Jean Maxwell's demands. Also, that it was she who was keeping the Devil at bay from her. Farmer Frances Scott was made of sterner stuff. He saw through the nonsense and bullying of his servant and brought the law.

Jean Maxwell was arrested and put into the tolbooth of Kirkcudbright parish.

> At Kirkcudbright 21st day of June 1805 at the Assize court. Did make choice of Alexander Melville of Barwhar to be their chancellor, and William Mure

> Factor for the Earl of Selkirk, to be their Clerk; and having confided the Indictment raised at the instance Robert Gordon, Writer in Kirkcudbright, Procurator Fiscal of court for his Majesty's interest against Jean Maxwell, present prisoner in the tolbooth of Kirkcudbright, the panel, with the Steward Deputy of the Stewartry of Kirkcudbright theron, adduced, they unanimously find the said Jean Maxwell guilty of the crime charged against her in the said Indictment.

The verdict was sensationally published on broadsheets.

> The Verdict... against Jean Maxwell, the panel whereby she is found guilty of pretending to exercise WITCHCRAFT, SORCERY, INCHANTMENT, and CONJURATION, and of undertaking to tell fortunes, contrary to the Enchantment and Provisions of the Act of Parliament passed in the 9th year of the Reign of King George II...
>
> The said Jean Maxwell to be carried back from the Bar to the Tolbooth of Kirkcudbright and remain for the space of a One While Year without bail, and once every quarter of said year, to standopenly upon a Market day in the pillory... for the space of an hour.

Thus, the sentence was carried out. Jean Maxwell spent her unhappy year in jail. But her stupidity and criminal bullying could have resulted in a much worse scenario had it been seventy years earlier. The guilty verdict would have seen her burn like the many thousands before her!

I finish this late Witchcraft trial with an earlier letter of 1758 from the Journal of the Reverend Mr Wesley in Sunderland. With the repeal of the Witchcraft Act, the Clergy lost their powers over their congregations. To preach by using fear creates a great bond to the Church. Without it, for the next fifty years after the repeal of 1736, ministers berated from pulpits the unjustness of the Act, as this following letter dictates…

> It is true likewise of that the English in general and indeed most of men of learning in Europe have given up all accounts of Witches and apparitions as mere old wife's tales! I am sorry for it, I willingly take this opportunity of offering my solemn protest against it.
>
> Giving up belief in Witchcraft is in effect giving up on the bible.
>
> Rev Mr Wesley … May 25th 1758

Source

The remarkable trial of Jean Maxwell, printed by Alex Gordon (1805)

CHAPTER 18

THE KIRKLISTON HEART ATTACK!

To the West of Edinburgh lies the Parish of Kirkliston. In 1655, it consisted of three great turnpikes traversing the parish, that between Edinburgh and Glasgow by the way of Bathgate, that between Linlithgow and Falkirk, and that branching between Kirkliston and Queensferry. The village was described in *The Statistical Account of Scotland* as, "having some good and modern houses but having a squalid appearance." The parish population is described as a few hundred souls in 1655, and this is where our next story stems from.

Within the many thousands of Witch trials that construct my library, it's hard to bring to the reader an original somewhat different case without repeating the same old methodical system of accusation, torture, trial, and burning, which gets repeated over and over again to the point the reader, once horrified, gets bored. This case in Kirkliston holds great detail from the works of George Sinclair's *Satan's Invisible World Discovered* (1685), but it does have an unusual ending for our victim, which I feel deserves some attention. I relive the trial records here…

A Mr William Barton had been accused of Witchcraft by the parish at Kirkliston. At first, naturally he denied everything, but after a spell with a torturer an unsettling confession was taken by him in which he testified that he had engaged in some casual sex with an attractive woman on the road from Kirkliston to Queensferry.

He met the fair maiden at Dalmeny Muir, who he described as, "a young gentlewoman beautiful and comely." He approached her, and at first, "she shunned his advances and the company on the journey he offered. When he insisted, she became very angry but at length she became better mannered towards him and eventually familiarity came so that they did embrace romantically and did what Christian ears ought not to hear!"

After this, he states, "he parted very joyful and arranged to meet the woman next day at night time." All was going rather well, but then, "He became sensible that she was the Devil! And she renounced his baptism from him and took him into her service. She then gave him a new name calling him 'John Baptist' and then gave him a Witches mark and £15."

In the Edinburgh tolbooth jail, he pondered his wanton lust and betraying of his own wife, calling out, "If I had twenty sons, advise them to shun the lust of uncleanness, I never saw such a beautiful woman maid nor wife but I did covet them which was the only cause that brought me to be the Devil's vassal."

In jail, one of the methods of his torture was sleep deprivation, and after he confessed, he begged to be allowed to sleep. His tortured body also had a tortured mind, and he aroused his jailers with cries from his nightmares... "He woke with violent laughter claiming the Devil had come to him and rebuked him with anger at his confession."

Edinburgh Tolbooth jail... Demolished in 1817

William's fate was sealed with his confession, he was to be 'wirret to death' (strangled) and then burnt at the stake.

The day for his sentence came. The baillies said to him his fire was built and ready, but William had a chilling reply of his own...

"I care not for I shall not die this day."

The executioner was sent for; it would be his job to lead William in chains and restraints through the crowd of abusive villagers venting their anger at a condemned Witch walking towards the stake. The stake where William Barton would be tied, strangled by a hooped rope tightened by a stick, as the wood and straw gathered to make the fire burned beneath him. Sometimes the fire took purchase too quickly and the victim had no time to be strangled properly, burned alive, and registered in the parish records as "BURNT QUICK!"

The executioner opened the jail door to fetch William to his doom... but the executioner, when seeing William all restrained by chains, took a step back, leant against the cell wall, held his chest and slowly slid down the wall till he was sitting... he was dead!

Today we would recognise the poor executioner's ailment as a fatal heart attack. Back in 1655, pandemonium broke out! Were not William Barton's words "I care not for I shall not die this day"? He had bewitched the executioner, and he had fallen dead! The executioner's name was Andrew Martin and with him was his poor upset grieving widow, Margaret Hamilton: "She clapped her hands and cried often." The baillies and minister saw fit to reward the grieving woman with the honour of strangling William Barton when he was attached to the stake. It would at least give her some piece of mind over her husband's death. To make matters worse, they even found William Barton's wife and she was now also accused of Witchcraft.

When they taunted William that he was still getting burned that day but by the executioner's wife, Margaret

Hamilton, he cried out, "How hath the Devil deceived me, let none ever trust his promises!"

William was led out and tied to the stake, and Mrs Margaret Hamilton, to the huge cheers from the crowd, strangled William like a professional. Then for an encore... she did his wife too.

They were both burned, with William's last words being he never knew his wife was a Witch. And his wife claimed she never knew he was a Warlock... nor did she know he was occasionally having sex with the Devil along the Dalmeny Muir road!

A further Witch was found in the Kirkliston area in 1661: August 20th, Jonet Millar was found. Other than her name, nothing more is mentioned of her.

The executioner's wife and William Barton's strangler was called Margaret Hamilton... today the most famous Witch in movie history is in the film *The Wizard of Oz*. The villain is the Wicked Witch of the West, who terrified me as a child! Who, would you believe, was played by the actress Margaret Hamilton (The Author has her autograph).

Sources

George Fraser Black, *A calendar of cases of witchcraft in Scotland, 1510–1727* (1938)

George Sinclair, *Satan's Invisible World Discovered* (1685)

Gazetteer of Scotland 1844

CHAPTER 19

THE LARGO WITCHES

Largo Parish Church-since 1243... this postcard photo taken around 1900

I have always tried to put a fresh perspective on the subject matter I write about. It is rather important to me when writing about periods of history to find the first source that covers the story; but also, to visit the sites in question and get a feel for when they were once a hive of activity. Old tolbooths and old ruined castles hide many a horrid story—especially when writing about old Witch trials in Scotland—and much can be understood about the history that took place here and further a story.

When researching, the first source to turn to for quality information is usually Parish Council records, or old diary accounts, or then maybe letters written by those who witnessed the trials. In this forthcoming account from my home village of Largo, I use all three and have the luxury of knowing two of the castles very well, being born myself in Largo. That Largo, sitting on the south-east coast of Fife, had a reputation for fairies and Witches may surprise many. I can guarantee the Witches of Largo have never made it into print or been examined properly apart from my interference. A lot of the information is incomplete, but there's enough to show the strength of the Church's reach towards Witches in its border, and some of the instances here stick in the mind, showing the Church at their most powerful, and also most ridiculous.

Largo, for such a small, populated area, has had its fingers in Scottish History from the early days of Roman occupation. Pictish remains and gold and silver treasures troves have been found, left and buried by a civilisation heaped in myth and wonder. Three lone standing stones are all that remain of their religion.

When King Alexander III died in 1286, the young heir, Margaret the Maid of Norway, died unexpectedly on her journey to Scotland. It left the calamity of twelve claimants to his empty throne. One of the claimants was an illegitimate child of King William of Scotland. He had married into a Largo family, taking on the name of Lundin in 1165. Robert De Lundin held an impressive castle (Lundie Castle) and vast tracts of land.

In 1490, another castle was built a half mile distant, to the east of Lundie Castle. Largo Castle was built on the grounds of an older settlement. It was traditionally used as a pleasant and safe ground to leave the Queens and Princesses of Scotland as the king and squires went hunting further east towards St Andrews. Whatever this ladies' retreat

What remains of Largo Castle is one single tower, it once had four. You can see how high the walls once were, at least 18 foot high.

looked like, it was lost when Largo Castle was constructed over it. King James III had granted this land to a great sea Warrior called Sir Andrew Wood who constructed this grand fortress of four giant towers where his descendants would live for the next two hundred years.

Now, half a mile north of this Largo Castle, another prominent 15th century build was Pitcruvie Castle, built by another branch of the Lundie family. All three castles governed Largo, and the Church in Largo held jurisdiction over them.

The first sign of Witches found in Largo is documented in the Presbytery records of St Andrews, where Largo Kirk came under its control. On the 1st of September 1598, the fear in the area from neighbouring villages finding Witches was all too clear as Burntisland and Pittenweem had recently found several and destroyed them. (See Chapter 22) The king, James VI, had visited St Andrews the previous summer (1597) and made a showcase of interviewing the many notorious Witches in the jail there before they were taken and burnt.

As this happened, Largo Parish issued a warning directed to the king...

> 1598 Sept 1
> We appeal to his Majesty King to cease travelling around the country of Largo as it is infected with the Pestilence of Witchcraft and the growth of Evil.

At this time, the king was travelling around Fife with a woman called Margaret Aitken who had been accused of Witchcraft in Balweary (ten miles from Largo). Her gift was being able to identify other Witches merely by looking at them! This the king was experimenting with her on his travels through Fife to the great panic of Largo Church (Margaret would be later confessed as a fraud, but not before many were put to death because of her accusations).

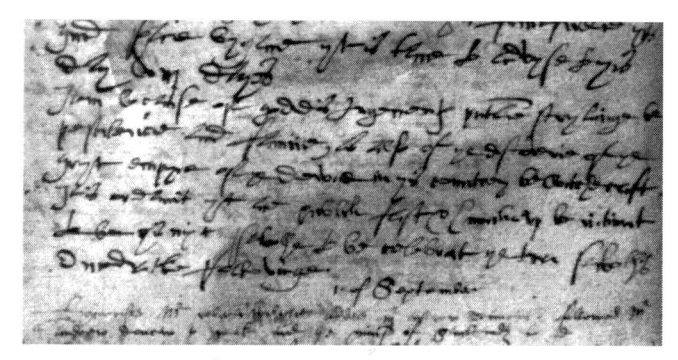

By August 17th, another warning (above) was declared as the fear of Witchcraft spread from village to village across the land. It reads,

> Item... because of God's judgements presently striking be pestilence and famine as also of the discoverie of the gryte empire of the Devil in this country be Witchcraft, it is ordanit that the public fast and humiliation be intimate this nixt sabbath immediately

But the Witch panic had set into Largo Presbytery...
In October 1603, the first Witches were found in Largo.

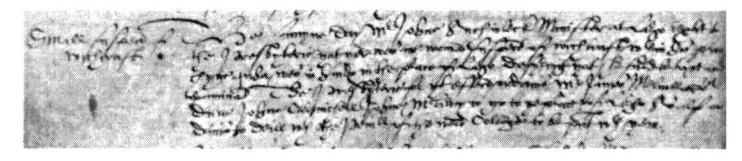

Jonet Small was accused. I give the parish ledger account above.

> Oct 20 1603... Small suspect of Witchcraft
> Mr John Auchinleck minister of Largo reported to

> the Presbytery that there was a Woman suspect of Witchcraft within the parish. Which is in the hands of the place of Largo desiring that she should be tried and examined. The Presbytery for that effect ordains Mr James Melville, Robert Durie, John Carmichael and John MacBirny to go to Largo as also ordained and the Dean of the new college to be present.

This procedure was followed by a further letter a month later...

> Nov 24 1603... Ordained the Commissioners appointed to try the Woman in Largo. To report their diligence that next day in that commission.

To commence trying a Woman for Witchcraft stemmed from Mary Queen of Scots 9th Parliament, sitting in 1563, when the Witchcraft Act was brought to law. This lengthy document states...

> It is statute and ordanit be the Queen Majestie and the thre estates foirsaidis that nae manner of person nor persounis of whatsoever estate degree or condition thay be of tak upon hand in ony tymes heirefter to use ony matter of Witchcraftis Sorsarie or Necromancie nor thame selves furth to have ony sic craft or knowledge thairof thairthrow abusand the pepill. Nor that ony persoune seik ony help response or consultation under the pain of deid as well to be execute again the usar as the seikar of the response or consultation.

To be caught practising Witchcraft in Scotland carried the death sentence. But also, anyone who has associated with a known Witch could now face charges. For the next 173 years, until 1736 when the Witchcraft Act was finally downgraded, over four thousand trials would have at least fourteen hundred Witches burned in Scotland. Witch trials became so common and troublesome that the names of the accused weren't even documented. Many trials just give a mention in the records, "some Witches burnt!" This is where researchers struggle to make a story out of the history as the trail ends abruptly. With the Largo Witches, due to letters written, we can illuminate the cases a little bit better, and although the history is still not completely clear on the result, we can account for some of the Largo cases, and others only imagine the fate they had!

What was applied during the incarceration of a suspect Witch was a rigorous torture by many ingenious methods. A confession was needed to complete the sentence, and of course other Witches could join the interrogation... all the parish courts needed was names!

What was found as Jonet Small was interrogated and the tortures started (possibly at Largo Castle, as it was three hundred yards from the church and had a good dungeon) was that a notorious other from Dysart (ten miles from Largo) called Agnes Anstruther had been aiding Jonet Small. Agnes had already been accused of Witchcraft in her own parish, and now she was accused by Janet Small as having "directed her in all she had done".

The Church decided to bring together Agnes Anstruther and Janet Small then have the parish confront the pair. This was to be done now at St Andrews. Meanwhile, another Witch had been identified in Largo from Jonet Small's ongoing interrogation. Beatrix Traills from Auchindownie (a farmstead in Largo) was now also accused of Witchcraft!

Beatrix Traillis was brought in to Pitcruvie Castle, (Auchendownie farm was a part of this castle's land). This area north of Largo Kirk was near an area long suspected for Witchcraft and Fairies—a dark forest called Keil's Den. The Den was a hollow U-shaped valley, thick with trees, and a burn running its length. Pitcruvie Castle sat on a hill at the top of the Den, the house of the Lyndsey family. It had a vaulted dungeon 10 foot deep that could only be accessed with a trapdoor at its roof, and the building was five floors high in a square-tower build. Prisoners would be thrown in head first and removed by ropes.

The Mysterious Fairy Bridge, an old 16th century traders' bridge in the valley down from Pitreavie Castle… an area long associated with Witches and Maleficarum.

This is where Beatrix would have been imprisoned. Soon after interrogation, her sister, Christian Traillis, joined her. The Presbytery was now to examine them, where the usual methods of Witch Pricking would be carried out. The Witch expert minister of Pittenweem, Nichol Dalgleish, was brought to carry out proceedings. He was bolstered with information coming of another Witch, this time from "the parish of Petmoge".

The growing group of Largo Witches were now: Jonet Small, Agnes Anstruther, Christian and Beatrix Traillis, and Alexander Martene from Petmoge. They were taken from Largo Castle to St Andrews where they would be interrogated in front of the Presbytery of St Andrews.

Pitcruvie Castle, as it once stood when built around 1400... and today.

Jonet Small was first arrested in October 1603. But by February 1604, five months had passed with the victims rotting in a St Andrews jail and no determination as to whether they were guilty or not! The patience of the master of Largo Castle was running thin. She was 80-year-old Lady Elizabeth Lundie, widow to Andrew Wood. She sent a letter to the parish in St Andrews…

> The Lady of Largo cravat the confession and depositions of ane against Janet Small with the Presbytery judgement there anent to be gevin to hir to the end she might know quether the said Janet deserves Death or nocht.
> ("the Lady of Largo wants to know the confession and charges against Jonet Small and the Church's judgement to know whether the said Janet deserves to be put to Death or not!")

The Parish Council answered,

> That quether the lay presents Jonet to an Assyse (court) that being required the Assyse will prove dispositions and judgement thereupon. Otherwise thought it not expectant to satisfy the lady's suit!
> ("whether the law presents Janet to the court, that being required, the court will prove judgement! It is not here to satisfy the Lady's demands".)

Basically, the Church was not there to satisfy a mere lady's request! But the elderly Lady of Largo was not giving up so easily. She persisted for information on Jonet Small's charges and sent two more similar requests… the chaos was just starting!

In the parish accounts for March 22, 1604, we find

a James Traillis now pulled into the investigation, likely a brother or father of the girls Christian and Beatrix sitting in St Andrews on Witchcraft charges. He was now questioned... "James Traillis satisfied the order of the Kirk and questioned and declarit his repentance in the face of the Presbytery to the great motion of all."

By October 11, the St Andrews Presbytery had had enough of the Lady of Largo and her non-stop letters. She was, because of her inquiries, now debarred from her own church! But this didn't stop her, she just kept the letters coming. She now filed a complaint asking why she had been debarred from her own church!

The minister of Largo, Mr Auchinleck answered,

> He did nothing but the command of the Presbytery, he approved his doing and was to bring said Lady Largo to acknowledge her faults ordains the process against Jonet Small is still to be recognised. The lady the nixt day is to be summoned to St Andrews. Mr Auchinleck being challenged by said Woman.

This 80-year-old woman was summoned to St Andrews, twelve miles distant, to answer for her imprudent letters! This was dangerous territory to walk on, it could be seen as Lady Largo defending the supposed Witch Jonet Small. To interfere in Church business and being female was an outrage in the Church's eyes. In the Witchcraft Act of 1563, it states a warning... "Anyone seik ony help response or consultation with any abusars or usars of Witchcraft under the pain of deid as well to be execute against the usar."

To involve herself in the care of Jonet Small could have Lady Largo accused herself of helping an accused Witch. The crime carried a death sentence and forfeit of land and property (something the Church would take a great interest in considering the Lady of Largo's huge estate). Worse was to come as she never appeared on the day asked. The parish account reads,

> Oct 18 1604 Lady Largo callit and compared nocht! Nor any in her name. The Presbytery recording the process orders the Lady to be warnit to the said day ("Oct 18 1604, Lady Largo called [to court] and never appeared, nor anybody representing her. The Presbytery records her to be warned on this day.")

A warning was sent to Largo Castle, with Lady Elizabeth's name on it, demanding to speed herself to St Andrews fast to answer the Church's demand. Again, she never appeared. The parish register notes,

> Nov 1st... Lady Largo callit nocht!... ordered to be with certification
> ("Nov 1st Lady Largo has not appeared... an arrest warrant has been issued")

The elderly Lady Largo, wrote back,

> Nov 18th 1604... Excuse hir nocht comperrance by letter because she was nocht able to travel to the Presbytery.
> ("Nov 18th 1604... Excuse her non-appearance by letter as she is not able to travel to the Presbytery.")

The Church's answer to that was to send a couple of heavyweight ministers to Largo Castle, James Melville and John Carmichael, to harass the old woman into subjection. This they managed to do by Nov 29th, when a broken Lady Largo, now realising her letters had put her entire estate in jeopardy, was now willing to beg for forgiveness for ever questioning the Church. The register reads,

> Nov 29th... The Commissioners directed to the Lady Largo declarit that she was willing to acknowledge hir fault and to make publick repentance. The Presbytery ordains Mr John Carmichael to receive her public confession and repentance nixt sabbath.

The entry for Dec 20th in the Parish accounts reads,

> Lady Largo—Mr John Carmichael report that the Lady publicly in his audience in the kirk made hir repentance—acknowledging and confessing hir infirmatie oversicht in seiking of hir health.

The poor 80-year-old had to prostate herself on her knees in front of the congregation, wearing nothing but a harsh gown of sack cloth to hide her modesty. Her insolence towards the Church's prosecution process towards a Witch was written on a board about her breast. She had to put herself at the utter mercy of the Church. Vulnerable and alone, luckily for her, her plea for mercy and forgiveness was accepted, and she finally disappears from the parish records.

As for the five accused Witches... over 12 months

passed in jail and still no court date to judge them was set. A description of jails at this time says of them…

> the lodgings are too bad for hogs and the food too bad for dogs… cold miserable disease-ridden areas.

It's no surprise a high percentage of people died because of the cold and filth inside the cells.

There is no record for the trial of the Largo Witches, or what happened to the Traillis sisters, but Agness Anstruther from Dysart, who had directed Jonet Small in her Witchcraft, appears in the St Andrews parish courts again on Witchcraft charges in 1613. This time they proceeded against her with the full force of the Church. She and another woman named Isobel Johnstone are named in the trial. Jonet Small seems to have been banished from Largo Parish, as in the church register it notes,

> October 11… Jnet Small… she fled the Parish and to his knowledge (the minister) she came nocht again, if she did it was in the elder's default to inform him.

There was another Witch found and arrested in 1644… Janet Wylie. Her story has been lost over the passage of time, but an English soldier wrote home saying that year he had witnessed, "over 40 fires burning Witches in the space of a month in Fife alone." Janet, with a high probability, may have been in one of them!

Another panic over malevolent beings in the village happened in 1653. The School Headmaster, living and running the School House on North Fues road, was brought to the attention of the St Andrews Presbytery. At this time, until 1872, Parish councils ran the schooling of children, so any wrong doings would be brought to the Parish Council very fast. Thomas Wilson was to be removed from his position as Schoolmaster and Teacher to the village for…

> Profanily taking the name of the Devil in his mouth, for tippling and taunting, and for not praying loud enough regularly every morning and evening in the School.

Thomas Wilson, "for not praying loud enough!", was forced to the pulpit and publicly rehearsed his faults, then confessed on his knees that God was righteous and desired other people to pray for him.

It seemed to do the trick, as we find in the parish register in 1670 his death is noted, and he is interred in between the graves of his two dead wives.

Photograph of the School building in 1890… it stands as a residence today.

CHAPTER 20

THE SUDDIE WITCHES OF MUNLOCHY

Suddie parish in 1699 was not a well place. A strange shadow had infected the land, and it was now seven years into a dark period of utter crop failure.[17] A gradual decline in the food chain had now reached its peak with people now dying in the streets of hunger. A third of the population would perish here.

The Parish of Suddie was abandoned in 1756... merging with Wester Kilmuir in a new Parish on the outskirts of Munlochy. Here, in the old parish, Margaret Provost, Margaret Bezok, and Mary Nicinnarich were accused of Witchcraft.

---

17. At this time in history, a violent volcanic action in Iceland was to blame for such a poor harvest in Caithness. In the author's lifetime a similar eruption in Iceland brought dusty deposits along car bonnets in Fife, three hundred miles south of Caithness.

Suddie, a small parish in Caithness, had its troubles; people from its parish in desperation were now reverting to the gods of old. A nearby sacred well in Munlochy, called a "Clootie Well", a place of tranquillity surrounded by trees, was where the stricken would go traditionally in pagan times to speak to the spirits of the well. It was reputed to cure illness. To wash in the holy waters, make an offering of coin, and leave a shred of clothing hanging from the tree nearby was what the spirits of old required. To leave a piece of clothes as an offering hanging from the branches was how your illness was taken from you… but to touch that piece of cloth again (or any others hanging), you would take the illness back with you.

The practices surrounding the Clootie Well highlight the superstitious nature of the area. It's against this background of woe that the superstitions of blame once again surface, and idle talk once again costs lives.

The Laird of Suddie was Captain Mackenzie, who was told that a certain citizen in the parish was a reputed Witch. Margaret Provost was the woman in question. Knowing the strange pestilence over the land, he had no hesitation in taking action against what may be the area's troubles. The laird with his servants broke into the Provost household; they rudely turned her out and reduced the house to rubble and ashes.

Within days, one of the servants who engaged in the burning took ill. His body swelled up to twice the size. Margaret Provost was thought to have caused the illness; her son came forward to say the man would get better only if another house was offered to Margaret!

Thomas Frazer, the minister of Suddie, now had a complaint from Captain Mackenzie; he too had suffered since he burned the house down. He had leapt a small stream and fell, injuring his leg—the stream not two feet across. This was enough in his mind to show that Witchcraft was afoot in the shire, and he wanted the minister to act!

Within no time, more accusations came… James Ned in Killern came forward with a story of Witchcraft involving Margaret and her daughter. He challenged her that, "James' Wife had skaith (injury) done to her by Margaret's hens." Margaret had threatened them that ill would come to them if her hens were injured.

Next day, one of James Ned's cows died, then a horse, then his plough horse took ill… then suddenly he took ill himself. It was seen as Witchcraft. It wasn't until Margaret Provost was officially challenged with being a Witch that the illness subsided.

More accusations came thick and fast as the panic and rumours of Witchcraft spread through the village, and others were accused.

Margaret Bezok, spouse to David Stewart in nearby Balmaduthy, was said to have threatened John Sinclair using a promise that she would overturn his cart… it indeed happened; and to follow, his own wife took ill. When Margaret Bezok was taken to see the stricken wife of Dave Stewart, she laid her hand upon her and miraculously she became well again as if the curse had been lifted.

Katherine Davidson in Balmaduthy said she was seen steering her cows away from Margaret Provost's evil hens, then said Margaret took offence and uttered wicked oaths. Soon, one of her cows died overnight and another had "brake his bones". Katherine had two witnesses against Margaret Provost in her threats—recorded as being Janet Urquhart and Agnes Davidson.

Another poor woman joined the accused. Murrock (Mary?) Nickinnairich in Kilearnan had threatened Alexander Maclay because his cattle had strayed across her land and were eating her meagre supply of corn in the field. The report says, "she repented at him, threatening him at a high rate." In a short time, he fell with an unnatural sickness that lasted 5 weeks. He was disabled with the illness until Murrock was brought to the house to remove the curse. When drinking a cup of milk from her, he immediately recovered.

Alexander claimed to the minister he had also witnessed a row between Murrock and two other women in the village. He heard Murrock say, "none of them would stand where they were for long." Both died within a short time!

Lastly, evidence came from John Maclay in Redcastle, saying he too had suffered bewitchment from Murrock Nicinnarich when he challenged her to the cause of his brother's sickness. He became seriously unwell until the Witch was challenged by the Kirk.

The three women, it seemed, were to blame for all the area's woes. The charges were afire with gossip and spite that a cause for all the ruined crops and misery had been uncovered.

Margaret Provost, Margaret Bezok, and Murrock

Nicinnarich would have been tried at Fortross, where the charges from Suddie parish were put to them. The trial doesn't exist anymore on record. Only a manuscript held in the University of Glasgow from the Boyd family of Trochrigg tells of the disturbance. With the upcoming Jacobite rebellions in this area, many documents were destroyed and lost in the confusion and upheaval. But it's with a fair degree of accuracy, reading the accusations and the fever of superstitious revenge, that an answer for the area's shortfalls and starvation had been found with the capture of the three Witches. Many others were burned as Witches for much lesser claims put against them. Although nothing exists of the outcome, I feel the three women were burned.

Sources

The information for this piece was found among the Papers of Boyd of Trochrigg, University of Glasgow.

Additional volcanic info was from: Bruce B Bishop, *A Brief History of Moray and Nairn*, Moray and Nairn Family History Society (2011).

Clootie Well info from Lesley Anne Brewster... High Priestess of Gardnerian Wica.

Bargarran House

CHAPTER 21

PAISLEY
THE BARGARRAN WITCHES

I bring you now a customary tale for its time. A tale of utter wickedness from 1697, where the rants of a small child would stand tall in the high courts of Scotland to cloud and confuse the rational minds of educated men. Because of a spoilt child in Paisley, twenty-one people would be accused of Witchcraft and seven would be condemned to the flames.

Paisley, in 1696, consisted of one main street half a mile long with some wynds and lanes spreading out from the main road in different directions. It had one church and a weekly market. In all, it was described by the solicitor Hamilton of Wishaw as, "a well-built little town plentifully provided with all sorts of grain, fruits and coal. A very desirable place to live." The census in 1695 noted that it had 2,200 residents.

A mile from the ancient church stood the house of Bargarran, run by the Shaw family now for three hundred years. They, like all notable families, had taken the name from the surrounding area, the area of Bargarran. The Shaws were hard-working lairds of good arable farmland, with six servants helping run the household. The peace and tranquillity of freshly tilled fields and market life was soon to be shattered by a commotion in the Shaw household.

Bargarran House stood on a flat stretch of land. The house itself was built in the 15th century. It had one grand entrance leading into the big, vaulted kitchens, a spiral staircase took you up to the great hall and living quarters, and further to the attics were the servants' quarters. The Shaws had five children: John, James, Christian, Elizabeth, and Jean, with six servants: two men, three women, and a herder in charge of the stables. The trouble at the Bargarran house started on the 17th August, 1696.

Katherine Campbell, a servant at the Shaw's house for many years now, awoke early with a thirst. She quietly went down the stone stairs towards the downstairs kitchens and was about to break the cardinal rule of a servant: you don't take anything without asking!

There was a good measure of milk sitting in the pantry where Katherine helped herself. But Katherine was not alone! A single figure came out the shadows to catch the milk thief "red handed"—eleven-year-old Christian Shaw, the master's young daughter. Katherine's crime was retold to Christian's mother, who later scolded the young servant in front of the other staff members. Milk was a treasured commodity, and although the Shaw household had some rents from the land they owned, they were in no way a rich household. Everything had to be accounted for, and so Katherine Campbell was shamed in front of her fellow workers.

Once alone, Katherine flew into a rage at the child, saying three times to her, "the Devil harl (drag) your soul through hell!" Christian retreated to her room in tears, and in the darkness of her room planned a fearsome revenge.

On Saturday 22nd August it started! The Shaws were entertaining guests when Christian became ill, gasping for breath and screaming out, "help, help!" Her parents ran to her aid, and in her bed, she leapt up and jumped the bed head and would have smashed her own head against the wall had someone not restrained her. Her own father put her into bed where she was now stiff as a corpse but her eyes still open and staring. An hour went by, then the silence of the night was shattered as she erupted into fits and screams that carried on at half-hour intervals.

A doctor from Paisley was called for. Dr Johnston applied several medicines and let blood from her, and it's here her illness takes a sinister turn. She now fought out at invisible demons, thrashing about defending herself as her father and doctor fought to restrain her. She let out piercing screams that, "they were trying to kill her." She named them as the servant Katherine Campbell and a local beggar woman Agnes Naismith.

Doctor Johnston could do nothing, so an older, more experienced Doctor in Glasgow was consulted. Christian was taken on the 31st December to Dr Mathew Brisbane's surgery where he writes,

> When she was first brought, she appeared so brisk in motion, so florid in colour, so cheerful in every way healthy he could hardly be persuaded she had need of a physician. But within ten minutes he was obliged to alter his thoughts. She rose from her seat and he observed her have a fit, she was taken by horrid convulsive motions and heavy groans into expostulatory mourning against some women.

The Doctor and her father witnessed her throw up balls of wet horse dung; feathers then appeared and lumps of coal, and even pins!

She cried out that her invisible tormentors were Naismith and Campbell once more. She stayed at the Doctor's for ten days as he worked on her. She was then sent home, where she was fine for two weeks, then again, the fits started, throwing up candle grease, eggshells, and more feathers.

This time she accused all the household servants of planning to drown her down a well. On the 11th of January, she was swept out of her chair in front of her parents and others, "as though she was caught in a whirlwind, along the hall she flew to the sound of her own manic laughter… her feet not touching the ground!"

On February 5th, the Presbytery now intervened, arresting the beggar Agnes Naismith and Katherine Campbell on charges of Witchcraft. In their examination, the Privy Council now considered the case as good a commission to try the pair with all the powers of the courts. Before long they had many suspects in the Renfrew prison. In total, twenty-six persons were arrested.

The town jail had been built in 1670 and it doubled as the Town Hall. Here the accused Witches were interviewed and strip searched, looking for marks the Devil had put upon them to baptise them into his fold. Marks like moles or warts were seen as this evidence, and before long, many had been found on the accused. There was much debate over using a Witch Pricker; these dubious people had proven false money grabbers in the past, casting many to the fires in wasteful greed of coin. But an old man was found who had some experience of being a Witch Pricker's

The town hall originally used as a jail, built 1670, demolished 1880.

apprentice and was set to work on the victims in the town jail.

Lord Blantyre, Frances Montgomery of Giffen, Sir John Maxwell, and Sir John Houston were the judges appointed to the case, but they now also had the opinions of fifteen local ministers who found time to observe the proceedings and wave Bibles around, influencing the proceedings. The judges put forth a statement after the evidence was represented against the accused: "Testimony that the malefices libelled could not have proceeded from natural causes and the prisoners were the authors of the malefices". Five prisoners had confessed the guilt through torture, and two others were found guilty by the Judges.

- John Lindsey... a Cottar,[18]
- James Lindsey... a Cottar,
- John Reid... a Smith,
- Catherine Campbell... servant,
- Margaret Lang... Wife to William Semple... Cottar,
- Margaret Fulton... servant,
- Agnes Naismith... beggar.

Before the executions on the 21st of May, John Reid managed to commit suicide in his own cell. The others were taken from the jail to a waiting scaffold and pushed from a ladder to hang, then cast down into the flames of a waiting fire beneath them... some were burnt alive!

The Bargarran house was demolished in 1800s. A memorial spot today marks the burning place of the Bargarran Witches

---

18. A "Cottar" was a labourer occupying a cottage in return for labour

Christian Shaw was never troubled again with her fits and aliments. She grew up in the Bargarran household and eventually, at the age of thirty-two, married a minister, the Reverend John Millar in 1719. He was the minister of Kilmaurs in Ayrshire. The marriage was doomed, as two years later he took ill and died. Christian moved back to Bargarran house and kept herself busy with her mother's help, spinning wool to manufacture a fine thread. She obtained some spinning machine at use in Holland and modified it to produce a fine beautiful thread.

In 1686, King James III passed an Act in his first Edinburgh Parliament called the "Act for burying in Scots linen", which was ordained to give the linen industry a boost. It was now law that: "no person whatsoever of high or low degree should be buried in any shirt, sheet or anything else except linen spun within the kingdom under the penalty of 300 Scots pounds." These sheets were known as "Winding sheets".

This Act and fresh English trade made Bargarran thread well known within the country and much sought after. It made Christian very wealthy and developed the "Paisley pattern"—a pattern of a curling pheasants feather that was the house symbol and is still in fashion today!

Christian would marry again in 1737, to a William Livingstone from Edinburgh, who was a prosperous Glover. But it seems Christian, at fifty years old, passed away in the same year. A grave stands in Edinburgh Greyfriars Cemetery for "Christian Livingstone, died 8th September 1737," and it says she had four children: Elizabeth, John, James, and Jean.

The first written works about the Bargarran Witch hunt came out in 1698: *Sadducismus Debellatus*. More written works followed. In 1785, *The Imposter of Bargarran* would stir interest in the case, and more writers would take notice, investigating the now empty household. Two writers in 1800 studied the empty building and found at the bedroom where Christian stayed—a loose brick behind, in the wall, where the bed once rested, it held a cavity… enough to hide coal, feathers, and dirt and be secretly obtained with one hand under the bedcovers?

On the base of Christian Livingston's gravestone there are two supporting carvings into the base of the stone. A skull and cross bones representing death as tradition allows, but for someone who was directly responsible for seven deaths on charges of Witchcraft, the left side carvings show two brooms crossed over. The traditional transport of a Witch! Is this mocking the dead or a statement from beyond the grave?

Sources

Sadducismus Debellatus Or, A True Narrative of the Sorceries and Witchcrafts Exercis'd by the Devil and His Instruments Upon Mrs. Christian Shaw. (1698)

Hugo Arnot, *A Collection and abridgement of celebrated criminal trials in Scotland from A.D. 1536 to 1784: with historical and critical remarks* (1785)

A History of the Witches of Renfrewshire printed by J.Neilson (1809)

Sharp, *Witchcraft in Scotland* (1884) p.171

The grave in Edinburgh's Greyfriars cemetery of Christian Livingstone, with two interlocking brooms... is it mocking the seven dead Witches she was responsible for killing?

Watson, *Narratives of the Suffering and Relief of a Young Girl in the West* (1698)

David Cook, *Annals of Pittenweem* (1867)

J.Mitchell and J.Dickie, *The Philosophy of Witchcraft* (1839)

R. Chalmers, *Domestic Annals from the Revolution to the Rebellion of 1745* (1861)

Pittenweem

CHAPTER 22

PITTENWEEM WITCHES (THE WEEM WITCH)

This chapter has a connection to St Monans in Fife, where we have the sad story of Maggie Morgan.[19] In 1650, a spurned lover, a man with influence, reacted to his refusal by calling sixteen-year-old Maggie a Witch. Within two weeks, the minister, to appease this great landowner, had her burning on a pyre at the back of his church on trumped up charges of Witchcraft. In her torture process, she mentioned a man who was said to be a wizard living nearby in Pittenweem… this man was called Thomas Brown.

With matters taken care of in St Monans, the ashes of the recent fire were put to nothing but memory. Maggie herself would over the years be completely forgotten about—even the trial records would vanish. But the stigma of being associated with Witches, or the whispers of being called one yourself, took more than just years to cleanse from your reputation. Fifty-four years later, in 1704, the repercussions of the St Monans Witch hunt would reach out its bony fingers and drag more innocent people into the plughole of death and despair once more.

On the 1st of April 1704, one of the high-profile women of Pittenweem was marched kicking and screaming into the tolbooth jail by armed guards. They put her legs in wooden restraints, and she sat down on the cold, stone floor like a common criminal. She was still shouting and

---

[19]. See Chapter 27 for more details

screaming as they closed the door on her, with now half the street's occupants coming out to see what the fuss was about. Beatrix Laing was in the jail... on charges of Witchcraft!

Beatrix was married to one of the ten Pittenweem councillors (called a baillie). The minister acted as head of the parish council and would have the respect of all. The councillors dictated the taxes and laws concerning Pittenweem. William Brown's position in the Council was as the town Treasurer when the baillies met once a week, otherwise he was a hard-working tailor who owned his own shop and several properties in the town. To his horror, the noise and wailing coming from the town jail was from his own wife, and to hear charges of Witchcraft go against her made him aghast of the consequences this charge may bring. After all, Queen Mary's 1563 Witch Act said that anyone found to be associating with a Witch could be classified as one also!

A sixteen-year-old blacksmith in the town had an argument with Beatrix—she, thinking her well-to-do position should have her served before his other customers; he refused! A full blown row started, and she foolishly left his Smithy and placed a wooded beaker with a piece of coal and some herbs at the boy's front door... a curse! The boy fell ill immediately. The minister was called and, in his wisdom, declared the boy bewitched. The young blacksmith gave Beatrix's name as his tormentor, and she was arrested and charged with using Witchcraft on the boy.

Now the torture started. To find conclusive proof of a Witch you had to have a confession from the suspect, and torture could get it. They had to have a confession using torture then a separate confession without torture. Both the confessions would lead to the Privy Council making a decision, or lacking that, on a unanimous vote, they submitted the evidence to the Parliament courts for a verdict.

It was commonly known that a Witch who went into the Devil's service would be given a baptism mark from the Devil himself. It would appear as a wart, a mole, or a third nipple. If this was not found on the body, the hair was shaved off to look through the pubic area and head. Again, if not found, it was thought to be under the skin! Here was where a Witch Pricker would be brought in.

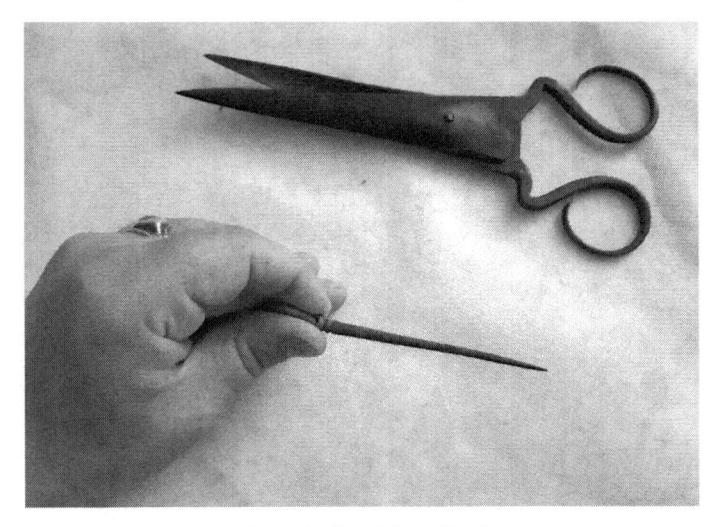

The Witch Prickers Tool

The Witch Pricker was a skilled torturer who would be looking for an invisible mark under the skin. He was looking for a spot on the body where the Devil has touched and given his own baptism mark, a mark that was now insensible to pain! The four-inch metal pricker was continually inserted into the flesh, and if at some spot the victim never cried out in agony, that was as good as a confession—the Devil's mark had been found! That was conclusive proof from the skills of a Witch Pricker, a Witch was discovered among them.

Here is a letter written by William Brown about his wife's treatment…

> She would not confess she was a Witch and in compact with the Devil, she was tortured by keeping her awake without sleep for five days and by continually pricking her with instruments in the shoulders and back until blood gushed put in great abundance so that her life was a burden to her, they asked her to confess to rid herself of the torture.

Finding a spot with the Witch Pricker's expertise was considered conclusive proof they had a Witch in their midst. But the Witch Pricker never got paid by the hour, he got paid per Witch; £6 was the fee for every Witch found, which was a huge sum of money at the time (the Treasurer of the town got paid £10.15 shillings per annum). It was in the Pricker's interest to produce as many Witches as possible, so it's no surprise that Beatrix broke down with the torture and confessed… giving more names of other Witches in the town.

More arrests came: Isobel Adam, Margaret Wallace, Mrs White, Margaret Jack, Nichol and Thomas Lawson, Janet Cornfoot, and a man named in the St Monans case fifty-four years back... Thomas Brown! And so, the Witch Pricker started to earn his fees, and the screams echoed around the town from the tolbooth rooms... night and day!

With the confessions signed, they were sent to Parliament for them to read the evidence and make a judgement on whether they were Witches. The confessions came back... the judgement said, "release the accused immediately as we see there is insufficient evidence to portray them as Witches."

The Pittenweem minister Patrick Coupar was furious. He was not to be denied, and he had the Witches tortured again to get further confessions. In this process, old Thomas Brown, in his eighties and accused all these years ago in the Maggie Morgan trial in 1650, died chained to a wall, defiant till his last breath. He was given a topsoil burial outside town—his remains were to be added to a fire when guilty verdicts could be had on the other Witches. The minister's plan was to burn them all.

Minister Coupar's church sermons spouted venom and hatred towards the Witches. One of the accused, a woman called Janet Cornfoot, was accosted by a brutal mob, who took her from her guards and dragged her to the beach by her ankles while they beat her with sticks and stones. She was tied by ropes, hanged above the sea line attached to a ship's mast as they swung her into the cold sea on a January winter's night. Throwing sticks and stones at the hanging figure, the sport went on for hours with the whole village now down at the harbour. It lasted till the tide went out.

The minister watched as she was finally cut down—she was still alive! Some kind soul tried to take her into a nearby house and bandage her wounds. The mob, afraid the Witch was being saved, smashed the door in, broke it down to get at her, pulled her outside, and put the broken door on her, pinning her to the sand. In a mad frenzy orchestrated by the minister's words, "do with her what you will", they fetched boulders to pile on top of the door until her ribs caved in on her. They finally squashed the life from her.

But Janet Cornfoot's ordeal was not finished. A heavy sledge was brought forward pulled by a horse and dragged over her lifeless body. Slices of flesh came off her, and these trophies they took to the families of the other Witches in jail to taunt them with what was going to happen to their daughters and wives next! Janet's body, or what was left of it, was buried beside Thomas Brown in the topsoil, on the Western braes of the town, "with barely enough earth to keep the crows off."

The confessions came back from Edinburgh a second time… "Release the accused", the judgement demanded. With two now dead, an investigation took place on the madness that had happened there. But once released, the others were afraid and were subjected to abuse from their former friends. They all ran, disappearing from history… apart from Beatrix Laing. She was found dead in the streets of St Andrews, a waif and a beggar. When people about to help her saw her prick marks, no one was brave enough to help her, for fear of aiding a Witch.

The old Harbour where Janet Cornfoot was murdered by a mob of her own villagers

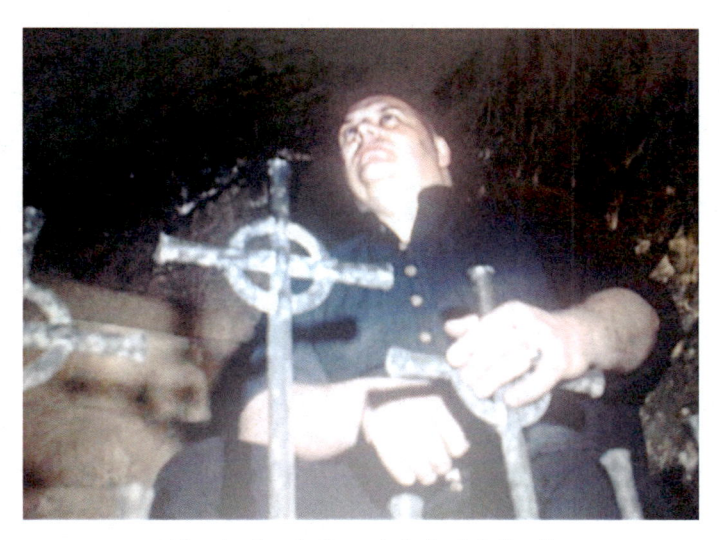

The Author in Beatrix Laing's jail cell

Sources

A true and full relation of the Witches of Pittenweem, Annon, printed by John Reid (1704).

Annuls of pittenweem, David Cook (1867)... (town council parish records, 1526–1793).

John Leighton, *History of the county of Fife*, vol 3, (1840).

CHAPTER 23

THE CAT HATERS
ISOBEL GRIERSON OF PRESTONPANS, 1607

Picture today your traditional image of a Witch. Old haggard woman with a broom and pointy hat, maybe a hairy chin, and of course, the black cat! It's the black cat we examine here, and one of the many Witch trials that had them used as solid evidence to declare a Witch found within a parish boundary.

The Church has always hated the feline creatures; maybe in response to the Romans feeding so many Christians to their lions for sport in their giant stadiums.

Pope Gregory IX, in 1232, declared: "Cats were evil and associated with the Devil and Witchcraft." For the next one hundred years, Christian followers killed mass quantities of cats! Perhaps as a result of this, the Bubonic Plague, spread by the fleas on rats and mice, ran unabated, with the rodents' natural enemy the cat in small numbers. Thanks to Pope Gregory, his actions helped kill one third of the known world population!

In St Andrews, towards the end of the summer, a festival of the "Cat Race" took place, with thousands of people lining the streets to watch a rope pulled across the road between the houses on either side. The rope was tightened, and from it dangled a small wooden cask, "like a man from the gallows". It was the sport of young men to ride horses beneath this wooden box and hit it violently with a club. The box contained a live cat. Every time it was hit, the poor animal screamed inside, and the bloodthirsty thousands cheered at the poor animal's hideous torture. This savage spectacle would escalate as eventually the box would break, plunging the cat below into the crowd. The poor animal was now thrown as high into the air as possible, the assailant receiving wounds from the cat's claws as it fought for life. The beast was grabbed and thrown into the air in this fashion hundreds of times until its demise… to the huge amusement of the crowd! The winner was the one who ended up with the dead cat.

St Andrews being the Archbishops residence, Pope Gregory's words were being honoured.[20]

This brings us to Prestonpans parish, in 1606, and Issobel Greirsoune. Issobel was married to John Bull, who was a workman on the salt pans (from where the town gets its name). Adam Clark, her neighbour for a year and a half, had complained of continuous bewitchery from Issobel. Every night, between the hours of eleven and twelve, Issobel Greirsoune entered his house "in the likeness of her own cat" and with others started up the most awful fearful noise of howling. His wife and servants were in great fear that they were to all go mad! The cats' howling brought the Devil into the house in the shape of a black man. The Devil assaulted the servants, pulling them from the floor by their hair and marching them up and down the house, as the cats serenaded him with their songs! This would render the servants ill for six weeks, unable to work because of the weakness put upon them by charms.

Another neighbour, William Burnett, it was claimed she punished by throwing a charm of a piece of raw enchanted flesh at his door. The Devil then appeared as

---

20. Although St Andrews did do horrid things to cats for sport in the old days, they are more sympathetic to them today. A big ginger cat called Hamish now has a statue to him. Known as a friendly fellow, he freely roamed the town and welcomed everyone. He became so well known a best-selling photo book was written about him, and the Hamish Foundation, founded in his memory, supports charitable projects around the town.

a suckling child and screamed at his fireplace for a year and a half. The Devil then presented himself to them both as—would you believe it—Issobel Greirsoune herself! It was too much for William Burnett who wasted away and died under this torment.

Another came forward in the trial with evidence; Mr Robert Peddan from the village of "Pauns". He owed the Witch Issobel 9 shillings and 4 pence. But he found when she walked through his brewery looking for a missing cat, she had turned his good batch of new ale brewing into "gutter-like dirt with a thick like pestilent odour" so that no man could drink it! Next, his wife Margaret Donaldson became ill when Issobel spent time with her. She flew out of bed hurting her shoulder to the point of feeling faint. Miraculously, she got better when Issobel had a drink with her... but afterwards, hearing they slandered her name as a Witch, Margaret became wasted and died ten days later. All was blamed on Issobel.

The evidence was too much against her... her trial was short in which it was declared she had the gift to put on and take off sicknesses. She was strangled and burnt on the Castlehill in Edinburgh, March 10th, 1706. All her moveable possessions were sold to pay for her burning costs! Note... In 2004, Mr Froome, the currant hereditary incumbent of the Baronial court of Prestongrange (Dr Gordon Prestongrange) exercised his legal authority to pardon the eighty-one Witches and their cats who were executed in the area between 1590–1679. It was his last act before the Baronial Courts were stripped of power!... Issobel Greirsoune was one of this number.

Sources

Robert Pitcairn, *Criminal Trials in Scotland from 1488 to 1624, Embracing the Entire Reigns of James IV. and V., Mary Queen of Scots and James VI. With Historical Notes and Illustrations* Volumes 1–2 (1833)

"Witchcraft in Scotland" in *Tait's Edinburgh Magazine* Volume 3 (1836), pp17–26.

CHAPTER 24

PERTH
THE MYSTERIOUS MAGGIE WALL

Perthshire is really the great gateway to the Scottish highlands. It has a circumference of forbidding mountains guarding the entrance through to Northern Scotland. The shire here is made up of many parish lands, Abernethy, Auchterarder, Crieff, and Dunblane, just to name a few, sitting together in this close proximity. But in the village of Dunning, another of the parishes of Perth, stands a strange, lonely monument... a twenty-foot high cross. It says in crude painted words: "MAGGIE WALL BURNT AS A WITCH 1657". To here now we unearth the mystery of Maggie Wall.

The monument is made from rudely carved stone blocks supporting a two metre stone cross. It seems to be early-1800s going by the manufacturing tool marks, but there is no history to it being built or by whom! A bigger mystery is that Maggie Wall doesn't exist on any parish register from the many parish lands around this area. More mysterious still is that Maggie Wall doesn't exist in any Witch trial records either. The conundrum is: who built it and who was Maggie Wall?

This isn't some random act of vandalism. The monument gets a fresh coat of paint and a wreath every year by a mystery source. It's now a bigger tourist catch than the 12th century church of Saint Serf nearby. The monument is one of a very few put up and acknowledged anywhere in Britain towards the forgotten martyrs of the Witch hunts. But Maggie Wall just doesn't exist in any record whatsoever!

A few years back, I approached Fife Council with a proposal towards a monument to the Pittenweem Witches—the twenty-six people who I wrote about in my book *The Weem Witch*. The Council was rather favourable towards the idea and offered land they held in the Pittenweem area for a memorial to go up. Pittenweem sits on a beautiful coastline, and a coastal walk exists for twenty miles in each direction from here. For the tourist, there are quaint churches to visit just yards from the sea, old historic remains of salt pan houses, windmills, harbours, and along this walk on the cliff top of Pittenweem would have stood my monument. It would stand yards away from where they killed the last of the Weem Witches, Janet Cornfoot in 1705.

I had backing from the ministers in Salem, who suffered a similar hunt just a few years before the Pittenweem hunt; they too crushed a Witch to death. The newspapers had a frenzy at my news, covering me in thirty editions up and down the UK, even papers in Poland! But all was to crash and fail. After Fife Council's cooperation, my next hurdle was the Pittenweem Community Council... over a thirty second phone call to the leader of the group, my proposal was shot down with, "No, we're not doing this!" I got the big newspapers involved and forced the Council to vote on it. They said they put out forms to all the households about a memorial and would hold a vote on it. I waited months for the result. "The result was a draw! (they declared, out of 1600 votes), so we're not doing it," said the Council with big grins.

That was that... end of story... except America had already pledged me £20,000 towards the monument from Scottish exiles and relatives of the Witches. I found that the great actor Sean Connery's ancestors were part of the mob that killed the last Witch in Pittenweem. The Salem minister's monument is a multimillion dollar tourist draw. But no, the Pittenweem Council thought otherwise. Three years later... three more pubs have shut in Pittenweem and another Hotel... the place has nothing but an excellent coffee shop (The Cocoa Tree) and one pub (up for sale) left for tourists. The place is almost a ghost town! With the Salem monument a big part of bringing in up to $299 million a year in tourism, it sickens me to think what difference my memorial could have made to this dying town.

Let's return now to the big stone monument dedicated to Maggie Wall in Perth. The big families around Perthshire who would act as baillies and judges in the civil courts were Strathern, Oliphant, Hay, Moncrieff, Drummond, and Rollo. Rollo would be the family holding the land the present monument to Maggie Wall sits on. But again, there is nothing about a Maggie Wall in any of the records; the name "Wall" doesn't pop up in any church register in the area. The "Wall" name is well established in the Orkneys and Ireland. But going through my Witch trial records, I did find something which may answer the question who was Maggie Wall?

There was a Witch trial in 1623 in Perth: a Margaret Hormscleugh, Issobell Haldane, and a Janet Trall were accused of Witchcraft. They were all over three months in jail and found guilty. Issobell Haldane was strangled and burnt on May 1th... Margaret Hormscleugh and Janet Trall were destroyed 18th of July.

A Scottish writer called Dalyell, wrote a book in 1834 about Scottish Witchcraft called *Darker Superstitions*, He wrote about the above Witch trial, reading from the parish Privy Council records. At a glance, the quill written records look like Janet Trall's name is read as Janet Wall. It's an easy mistake to make, and with a quill flick it does look like her second name is Wall! She was burnt with Margaret Hormscleugh. Dalyell printed the book and the details of the case, calling the woman Janet Wall!

The monument was constructed about the early 1800s Has some one read Dalyell's book and got the two Perth Witches mixed up... Janet Wall and Margaret Hormscleugh becoming "MAGGIE WALL"? Maybe the date 1657 is wrong? Is this finally how Maggie Wall is established—through an author's mistake?

There were many trials in the Perth area for Witches:

- 1580... Witch banished
- 1581... a woman summoned and warned for Witchcraft
- 1582... a witch in the Tolbooth
- 1588... Johnne Myllar and Meriory Blaikie for bewitching and killing William Robertson
- 1598... Janet Robertson, Marion Macause, Bessie Ireland... burnt
- 1612... Janet Campbell and (no first name) Robertson
- 1615... Marion Murdoch... complaint for Witchcraft
- 1620... James Stewart... suspected
- 1623... Issobel Haldane..Strangled and burnt
- 1623... Margaret Hormscleugh and JANET TRALL
- 1628... Bessie Wright
- 1643... Agnes Stoddart and Thomas and Jean Rob
- 1715... Sarah Johnstone and Margaret Ogilvy... burnt as Witches

One other Witch trial happened in nearby Dunning, in 1656, and is not recorded in the national records but recorded offhand in a publication called *Transactions, 1650–67* by the Bannatyne Club. Printed in Edinburgh in 1836, it mentions that "4 Witches were found in 1656 from the Parish of RedGorton." No other details exist about the case bar what is written here. No names either! The Witches would have been arrested in 1656, and one could have been named Maggie Wall! And they could, after the confessions and jail time, have been burnt as confessed Witches in 1657 as the monument suggests.

It seems unlikely we will ever know the truth, but whoever put the monument up deserves huge praise. There's a distinctive lack of tributes to those who suffered the awful Witch trials. I myself tried to get one put up, but the authorities failed my attempts. Like the Maggie Wall monument, I may have to do it myself... in secret!... watch this space...

Sources

J. Nicoll, *Diary of public transactions and other occurrences, chiefly in Scotland, 1650–67* (Bannatyne Club) (1836)

CHAPTER 25

POLLOCKSHAWS, RENFREWSHIRE, 1677
THE BEWITCHING OF SIR GEORGE MAXWELL

Sir George Maxwell held the Barony of Pollock. He had inherited the title from his relative Sir John Maxwell and had then been knighted by King Charles I. Sir George was a prestigious man well thought of on the court circuit. With Pollock owning the largest grain mill between Glasgow and Irvine, and now having good road access to the Glasgow sea ports, Pollockshaw was becoming a wealthy title to have.

On the 14th of October 1677, Sir George had been travelling through Glasgow when suddenly he took ill. He was taken back to his house in Pollock, and a surgeon diagnosed pleurisy and immediately started to bleed him. His illness carried on for seven weeks, when he was getting a sharp pain in his side. He now wasn't bedridden but was in so much pain he couldn't do his court duties and had to be housebound.

Before long, a deaf and dumb girl called Janet Douglas, a servant in the household, managed to explain by hand gestures that she knew her master's illness was because of Witchcraft. She took the son of Sir George to the house of the widow of John Stewart. Jonet Mathie was with her son, also called John, and her daughter Annabel, who was fourteen years. They were employees in the grain mill in the town. With a thorough investigation of the house, a strange picture frame was found hidden in a space behind the fireplace. It had a strange human figure in the frame made from bee's wax: the distinctive figure of a man with iron pins sticking out of the sides. With this suspicious item, Janet Mathie was arrested for Witchcraft and taken to Paisley tolbooth.

After the discovery of the picture frame with the waxen image, Sir George Maxwell recovered slightly from his illness. Then he relapsed worse than ever to the thought he was going to die! But John Stewart, Jonet Mathie's son, was then found to have his own image of a man, this time made of clay. It was obvious to the authorities that it coincided with Sir Maxwell's increased illness. They found the clay image among the boy's bed straw. The son and mother denied all knowledge of the images found in their house, but the authorities used torture on her, and she soon changed her story.

A man in black guise had entered her house with the clay figure. "It was the Devil", she said. He came with his coven of Witches, being neighbours Bessie Weir, Marjory Craig, Margaret Jackstone, and her brother John.

A Witch Pricker was sought by the court. The pricking was a supposedly fool proof way of identifying a Witch. Pins several inches long were prodded into the flesh. If a spot was found on the body where no pain was noticed, it was deemed "the Devil's mark". When this mark was found by a Witch Pricker, that was all the evidence they needed for a trial. After the Pricker started his work, soon her son John Stewart was found with "a great plenty" of the Devil's marks. He confessed that he and his mother with the others accused, were guilty of Witchcraft. Margaret Jackson, aged forty years, also confessed to a pact with the Devil and to making both the images. The Witch Pricker also found marks on her body.

On the 17th January, a third doll of clay was found under Jonet Mathie in her prison house in Paisley. Now the confession was that "the malice was against the whole family of Pollock, not just Sir George Maxwell".

A commission was granted to bring the six to trial in Glasgow. Sir Patrick Gauston, James Brisbane, Sir John Shaw, John Anderson, and John Preston, all exercised in the justice department for over six years, were to judge the case on the 27th of January.

Annabell Stewart, the fourteen-year-old daughter, confessed to "putting her hand on the crown of her head and the other hand under her foot and giving herself soul and body to the Devil's service. Her mother was promised a new coat to take the Devil's service, and then the black man had sex with her to cement the bond."

On the 15th of February, Jonet Mathie was secured to her jail cell floor by wooden stocks lest she try to harm herself—the stocks so heavy two men could hardly carry them. By morning, she had moved the stocks from one side of the room to the other, and she had released herself from them.

By the time the trial had reached this far, poor Sir George Maxwell had died. There now could only be one outcome.

She and the others were convicted of Witchcraft and taken to the Castle hill where they were strangled first and then burnt as Witches. The evidence was so great against them! The daughter Annabel was reprieved her sentence due to her young age and left to remain in the prison cell… what eventually happened to her is not noted.

The deaf girl Janet Douglas, who led the authorities to the house with the waxen images, now fell under suspicion. How did she know so much to identify the Witches? She was arrested and taken to Edinburgh Canongate jail and remained there six months to be examined. Miraculously, while there, she regained her voice. It was said she spoke in good Latin, a language she never studied! She became quite notorious, and persons out of curiosity would pay coin to talk to her, thinking she had special gifts that could expose love intrigues and fortunes. She was eventually released on 30th March 1679, "alleadged having ane familiar and consulter of spirits." She was banished from Scotland, meaning she was to be transported to the colonies.

Janet's story stops here. The transportation lists to the Americas and West Indies don't show her name. She may have never even reached the transportation ships. The Edinburgh Tolbooth was a notorious prison with terrible conditions. I fear after her long stay, she succumbed to illness and death not long after the trial.

Sources

George Fraser Black, *A calendar of cases of witchcraft in Scotland, 1510–1727* (1938)

Richard Bovett, *Pandæmonium, or the Devil's Cloyster. Being a further blow to modern Sadduceism, proving the existence of witches and spirits, etc* (1684)

Joseph Glanvill, *Saducismus Triumphatus Or Full and Plain Evidence Concerning Witches and Apparitions* (1700)

Charles Kirkpatrick Sharpe, *A historical account of the belief in Witchcraft in Scotland* (1884)

George Sinclair, *Satan's Invisible World Discovered* (1685)

Ruins of St Andrews Cathedral

CHAPTER 26

ST ANDREWS WITCHES

We now go to St Andrews for a most unjust and ridiculous story of Witchcraft. This tale is typical, where healers and advancing medicines were stalled by the Church in its fear of "wise women".

St Andrews, from its humble beginning, was formed as a religious centre of learning. It is also famous for its religious martyrs, who today have a rather splendid monument dedicated to them on the coast—a monument raised by ministers for ministers; ministers who threatened others simply by preaching from a different prayer book.

Their reward for preachers not conforming to the religion of choice was to be tied to a post and burnt alive. At the time they were branded in the courts as "Heretics", but the names of George Wishart, Patrick Hamilton, and Walter Mill are looked on fondly today by fellow Protestant ministers who raised this monument to their own kind. What is missing from this quaint, affectionate remembrance are the names of the other fifteen people who suffered likewise horrible deaths at the stake in St Andrews, branded Heretics also, burnt by the Church's authority as the martyrs were, but the crime of Heresy also covered the accusation of Witchcraft!

It saddens me greatly that these people today are ignored.

You now have to search hard through books and old files to find the names and stories behind the Witches burnt

The Martyrs Monument in St Andrews

in St Andrews, but today I give you the story of two of them: Alisoun Pierson and Agness Melville.

The Archbishop of St Andrews in 1588 was Patrick Adamson; he was not in the best of health, quite elderly, and exhausting doctors with his growing list of ailments. He had painful swellings of his legs—it was agony to walk—but he also had over thirty other Cardinals and ministers to govern over. The doctors used a method of "bleeding" him, cutting a vein to drain of what they thought was "bad blood" from his system. But this endless process was just making him weaker. He was now desperate, and one of his ministers from Anstruther came forward to say his niece was rather gifted in herbs and medicines and may be able to help!

James Melville was a minister in Anstruther who had lost his brother a few years back, and so looked upon his niece Agnes Melville with affection and care. He thought if she impressed the Archbishop with her medical knowledge, she would be well rewarded and put in good standing in the Church's eyes... what a terrible mistake!

Agnes Melville came to the aid of the Archbishop of St Andrews. She was in awe of the grandness of her surroundings: the Archbishop was one of the most powerful men of Scotland. For company, and to help her out, she asked a friend called Alisoun Pierson, living in the Byrehill area just outside the city, to help. It seemed Alisoun was actually the gifted one, and with her herbs and potions, she started to see results. After two weeks working on the Archbishop, he started to feel better... much better. By this time, Agnes took a back seat and left Alisoun to continue for the next few weeks working on the Archbishop, until he was totally cured!

Alisoun's next action would have life changing consequences for her and Agnes. After all the work she had done, she thought the least she deserved was to be paid for her tireless effort to cure Patrick Adamson. She meekly asked the Archbishop for a payment in coin for curing him!

The Archbishop, utterly ungrateful now he was back to his full health, reacted in anger, and in his furious state within a week Alisoun was thrown in jail on charges of

Witchcraft, and Agnes was right behind her. Alisoun was charged with "putting a hand on the Archbishop and taking his illness from him and by putting her hand on his horse, she transferred it to the beast which then died". Anybody who had consulted or previously worked with Alisoun was publicly whipped and flogged down the streets of St Andrews "for the actions of consulting the condemned". Alisoun was tortured and found guilty of Witchcraft and so was to be burned to death!

Agnes Melville was also accused, but miraculously, because of her Uncle's position as a minister and of him being a friend of the Archbishop, she was let off with a sound flogging.

But poor Alisoun Pierson burned. The ungrateful Archbishop stood and watched with the rest of the Clergy as Alisoun went up in flames. Friends who had also benefitted from Alisoun's skills, people who had associated with her, stood with raw backs from their floggings... they could do nothing to help her!

With modern interpretation of the Archbishop's ailments, it's clear he had what they called "Dropsy" associated with kidney problems or a sexual disease. Among the many herbs that Alisoun used on the Archbishop was the flower foxglove... two hundred years later, doctors experimenting with foxglove extracted a drug called Digitalis. It assists patients to pass excess water and salt from the body, an effective treatment today in heart patients. What Alisoun and Agnes used on the Archbishop were the precise medicines needed for his complaint... two hundred years before it became properly recognised. Had it not been for the constrictions of religion on medicine, as the above case is but one example, medicine today would be advanced by hundreds of years.

Agnes, now with an accusation as a Witch, couldn't go back home to Anstruther for fear of reprisals. She is recorded wandering in Berwick and Lundin Links, but in 1595, Agnes Melville's luck finally ran out. Her Uncle had died, and when she was seen again in Anstruther near the family home, she again was accused of Witchcraft. This time she had no one to protect her. People who had used her medicines and knowledge still had the flogging scars on their backs for associating with her. To see her back stirred sore memories. She was accused and arrested for Witchcraft. A poem was written…

> Ane Devil Duelling in Anstruther,
> Exceading Circles In Conceattis,
> For Changing Of Useless Meats,
> Medusas Crafts She Would Declair,
> In Making Adders In Her Hair,
> Medeas Practises She Had Plane,
> That She Could Make Old Men Young Again.

You can see the above poem strikes at her success in healing the Archbishop. The stigma of being tainted in a Witchcraft trial never left you… it took 7 years, and she was still reviled for practising Witchcraft!

Agnes burned at the stake on September 10th, 1595 with Elspot Gilchrist and Jonet Lochequoir. A girl with good intentions and herbal skills killed by the ungrateful regime of a religion she tried to help!

<

St Monans Church

CHAPTER 27

THE ST MONANS WITCH, MAGGIE MORGAN

Two weeks ago, I travelled along the Fife coastline, the still of the day had finally brought the right conditions I had been awaiting eagerly for months... thick fog!

I'm a lecturer of the strange and unusual, a Witch Historian, a writer that's not afraid to cover the darker side of History—subjects that are certainly unappealing to some. But as I trawl through history's bowels, I turn pages that I find utterly fascinating and yet I'm saddened how such rich stories have been forgotten. The tale I now give you is a romance that went bad. It's a small part of a much larger canvas, starting in a little, pretty fishing village, and from the actions here, people would be drawn into a plughole of torture, misery, and murder. The location I was heading to on this fog-smeared day was the village of St Monans and its parish church.

St Monans church dates back to the 14th century; it's been a Presbyterian place of worship since 1646. Its uniqueness is in its location, sitting just yards from the coastline. Our story of romance and woe starts from Oliver Cromwell's occupation of Scotland in 1651.

St Monans was a village that supported itself with fishing and weaving. The fishing people in a superstitious age risked their lives every time they took their boats to sea; so, as protection, they trusted nobody bar their own kind. People had lived among the St Monance natives for up to forty years and were still frowned upon as "outsiders". This stance saw them marry among their small group until the church was burying stillborn bairns at a regular rate.

One girl, Maggie Morgan, a pretty sixteen year old, surprisingly unmarried for her age, took the fancy of one of the local gentry, William Anstruther. His family had owned land here since 1066 when the Norman family of Candela arrived. It was customary for the Norman families to take up the name of the area they governed, so the nearby fishing town of Anstruther was where they took the name.

All seemed to go rather well with the romance; rides on gallant horses and elegant nights sailing with a background of the full moon. The proposal eventually came and frightened Maggie with the realisation of the gulf in class between the two. She spurned his advances and soon found solace in a common fisherman's arms. Within two weeks, the Anstruther heir had her declared a Witch, and the local minister, keeping favour with his great landowner, followed suit.

The St Monans jail, after damaged by fire in 1912.

Maggie was an uneducated girl, completely naïve, confused, and slighted by the fact she heard accusations "she was in compact with the Devil." She was imprisoned in a secure house, tortured using sleep deprivation, and beaten with an oar pierced by long nails called a "Witches goad". A horn was blasted in her face to keep her awake in exhaustion, while the minister demanded she sign a confession of guilt.

The Witches Goad used on Maggie Morgan.

With life now such a burden to her, friendless and so alone, she signed a confession. It claimed she had caused the death of someone at sea by stirring a cup in a barrel of water, and at the right moment, tipped the cup and sank it, uttering the words "mak yer bed among the crabs." The boat did likewise, drowning its occupant. She had also been accused of flirting with a known Warlock from nearby Pittenweem called "Cowzie, Brown of the braes", and having the ability to turn herself into a hare.

Her fate was sealed. The Laird of Anstruther's

influence, inspired by his rejection, had the good favour of a minister so willing to please.

On a fair June morning, young Maggie Morgan, who now had a child (but who's?) was brought forward to a stack of timber formed at the back of the church land. She was tied to a stake, strangled, and with the population of the nearby villages watching, she was burnt to ashes.

St Monans church has a unique solid sandstone structure, but the tall steeple looms high with a strange rim (like a Witches hat). The remaining unburnt bones and ashes of Maggie were shovelled into bags and emptied around the rim… to be blown by the wind into consecrated ground. Her story finished, and history forgot her. She doesn't exist on any record of the Witch hunts bar her first name and the year. It took an 19th century writer, writing one hundred and fifty years after her death, who accessed meagre town records (now lost), to briefly flirt with her story. He put it in a book selling one hundred copies. I have one.

What makes Maggie's story stand out is for what happened next! The stone was rolling, and from St Monans it would roll to the nearby town of Pittenweem, simply because a Witch from Pittenweem is named in person during the Maggie Morgan trial, where years later his name would resurface.[21] That is where a further story of draconian Witch hunts would escalate, drawing in another nine people accused of Witchcraft. It's where my previous book *The Weem Witch* really starts, giving the history of the 1704/5 Pittenweem case in detail. Maggie was not the first

---

21. See Chapter 22.

creature destroyed in this little village; two sisters Christian and Beaty Dote, in 1644, met the flames in the Pittenweem Priory gardens, burnt with several other Pittenweem Witches. Another is mentioned as "Tibbie Dowie" living around 1548, but nothing is mentioned as to her fate.

My day in the fog was to capture this tall structure in a haunting pose, this I achieved. Maggie's last resting place looms large. Today you can wander behind the church and stand on the area she met her death.

SOURCES

GF Black, *A calendar of cases of witchcraft in Scotland* (1938)

John Jack, *An Historical Account of St. Monance Fife-shire, Ancient and Modern* (1844)

CHAPTER 28

THE STRATHGLASS WITCHES, 1662

In 1640, the General Assembly of the Church of Scotland issued a statement: "That all ministers within the kingdom carefully take notice of charmers, witches and all such abusers of the people and urge the Acts of Parliament (Witchcraft Act of 1563) to be used against them." If the Witch hunts weren't at fever pitch enough in those "burning years", another declaration came in 1649, when the Church of Scotland demanded a nationwide fast, the reason being:

> The continuance and increase of sin and profanity, especially of the sin of Witchcraft. Witches are not to be sworn in at court. The point being as the Prince of Darkness was the only lord and master whome these persons professed to serve; it would be blasphemous as well as useless to administer to them the oath which Christians are considered to respect.

It's with this growing hatred that the Laird of Erchless Castle, Alexander Chisholm, in Beauly Inverness-shire, hatched a wicked and relentless action to rid himself of a Clan of Macleans who were tenants on his land in Wardlaw parish.

The Macleans had lived peacefully in the Strathglass area as farmers for over three hundred years. But Alexander wanted them removed. He knew legally he had no motive that a court would accept as justifying his actions. So, with Witch hunting at fever pitch in Scotland, he accused the Macleans of Witchcraft. He took fourteen of them into his own custody, separating the leader Hector Maclean from his kin, throwing him into the Inverness tolbooth jail.

Hector's brother, Donald Maclean, managed to escape Chisholm's clutches, and as the laird's men searched for him, he managed to compose a letter. He told of the wicked proceedings and addressed it to his clan Chief of the Macleans, a powerful chieftain on the Isle of Mull called Sir Allan Maclean of Dewart.

Alexander Chisholm took the fourteen women to his 16th century Erchless Castle where the vaulted dungeons awaited. The castle was an L plan four-storey tower building, with its original built from the 13th century, sitting eight miles southwest from Beauly. It was the seat of the Chisholms.

The newly arrived women went through a brutal set of tortures with the help of a mysterious Witch Pricker. The accused Witches had ropes tied to their thumbs by the Witch Pricker's two manservants. The ropes were thrown over ceiling beams and the poor wretches were hoisted off the ground to dangle in agony as thumbs dislocated and skin and muscle held the weight. Then fire was applied with torches to burn their feet. Others were tied to horses with ropes around their necks and feet and pulled around the castle grounds.

This Witch Pricker had travelled the area of Inverness-shire. In Elgin, two Witches had been tortured and burnt,[22] in Forres another two.[23] A woman in Inverness called Margaret Duff had also just been burnt. Now, here the Witch Pricker had fourteen subjects to practice on in the comforts of the castle. Two cloaked servants helped with the ropes and feet burnings. The Maclean women were also shorn of all their hair, brutally cut off with shears as to make a huge hedge which was thrown into a ditch.

The Witch Pricker had commissions granted from Edinburgh Privy Council to exorcise the women as Witches under the name of John Dick. He searched for the Devil's mark on their bodies under the hairline he had just removed, and before long, he had confessions from all of them, although some had died during the proceedings to get this confession.

Clan Chief of the Macleans, Sir Allan Maclean of Dewart, sent a letter to the Edinburgh Privy Council demanding justice for his people and explaining the circumstances. The Privy Council hastily withdrew the original commission and sent a letter demanding so to Alexander Chisholm.

---

22. May 7th Margaret Kellie and Barbara Innes were confessed guilty... both burnt 11th November.

23. Forres Witches: Issobell Elder and Issobell Simson... burnt at Forres, May 4th 1663, see Chapter 15.

Edinburgh Privy Council Order 3rd July 1662

    Annent a petition presented by Sir Allan Mclean of Dewart on behalf of his kinfolk…

Hector and Donald Maclean.
Janet Maclean, spouse to John Maclean,
Margaret Maclean, sister to Janet Nie Rory Voie,
Mary Nie Finlay Vic Comes,
Katherine Nyn Owan Vic Connoch,
Mary Dollor,
Katherine Nein,
Farquhar Maclean,
Cormyle Grant,
Mary Nein Goune,
Bakie Nein Ian Dowie Vic Finlay,
Christian Nein Farquhar Vic Ean,
Baikie McInch,
Mary Muarwrie Muish.

    Showing that Alexander Chisholm of Comer, Colin Chisholm his brother, John Valentine and Thomas Chisholm his cousins. Having conceived an inveterate hatred against the supplicants because he could not get them removed from his lands in a legal way. Whereof they have been most kindly tenants these 2/3 hundred years by past. They have been unjustly seized upon without any order expressly against the proclamation issued out by the Lords of the Privy Council. The women having been incarcerated in Alexander Chisholm's house and Hector Maclean in the Tolbooth of Inverness. A daily search is ongoing for Donald Maclean as he dare

> not keep his own house. All cruelly tortured, one has become distracted, one has died with torture more bitter than death itself.
>
> Desiring a warrant to the charge of Alexander Chisholm to present Hector Maclean and remnant of persons above to Inverness to the present Simon Frazer son to John Frazer of Glenvaickie and Alex Grant and Robert Winchester Burgess of Inverness.

Nothing more is written about the Strathglass Witches after this letter. From the lack of general information, we have to imagine that with the Clan Chief of the Maclean's influence, the women left alive were released from Erchless Castle and Hector Maclean from the Inverness tolbooth jail.

The Witch Pricker would move on to other villages and again find more Witches. One was found in Dornoch, a man called John Hay. He was pricked and found guilty, but the Dornoch Parish, wary at the ease this Witch Pricker was finding Witches and the massive expense on the parish's finances, refused the application. Mr Dick (some reports "Dickson") the Witch Pricker then sent sixty-year-old Mr Hay to the Edinburgh tolbooth 180 miles away under armed guard. The Magistrates there were amazed at his brutal treatment and demanded the arrest of Mr Dickson.[24]

---

24. This intriguing character, Mr Dickson (some records such as "Fraser Chronicles" call him by mistake "Mr Patterson"), a brutal torturer leaving many in his wake dead was surprisingly unmasked as a woman in disguise! She has a chapter in my previous book *Scotland's Untold Stories*, Chapter 8, "There's something about Mr Patterson".

SOURCES

James Fraser, *Chronicles of the Frasers 916–1674*, (1905).

CHAPTER 29

THE TORRYBURN TERROR

The Inauguration of Lilias Adie, the Toryburn Witch

As the new century turned over, leaving the dark days of the Witch hunts behind in the blood-stained 17th century, England questioned the rationality in the persecutions and restrained themselves from the time and expense of bringing a Witch to trial. Scotland's lawyers also were slowly becoming wise to the evidence of lying children's accusations and foolhardy superstition, finally, actually questioning the viability of it. But on the east coast of Fife, the Witch hunts carried on in bloody earnest.

In 1704, the Parish of Pittenweem, run by a mad minister with all the zeal of ministers during the heights of the 1600s Witch hunts, accused nine people in his parish of Witchcraft and brought death and destruction to his flock once more. Along the Fife coast, in the village of Torryburn, another insane minister at the same time as the Pittenweem hunt, screamed from his pulpit in church that his land was infested with the acts of the Devil. He too found a victim... poor confused, old Lillias Adie.

Torryburn is bounded by the parish lands of Culross on the west and Dunfermline to the east. It had a small harbour in 1704 but not sufficient enough for a fishing fleet. The town sustained itself with several coal mines, salt pans, and a cottage weaving manufacturing business.

A local woman called Janet Bizet took ill. During a drunken night with friends, she warned her illness was orchestrated by a local woman called Lillias Adie. Agnes Henderson soon spread the story. She confessed she heard Janet Bizet cry out, "O God, O Christ, here is Lilly Adie coming to take me! Oh, keep her from me she is coming." Others like Jean Wilson (in some accounts named as "Neilson") came forward to declare they had been bewitched also. The town Baillie, Mr Williamson, brought up the complaint at the next Kirk session, and Lillias Adie was arrested on charges of Witchcraft, at ten o'clock at night on 28th July!

Torture was applied to Lillias Adie, and by 31st July, a sinister story was produced... She had met the Devil during the harvest at a place called the Gollet between Torryburn and Newmilne. At this location, the Devil had taken her baptism rights from her and had for her his own initiation for a Witch into his service. He held a ceremony putting his hand on the crown of her head and the other on the soles of her feet, and with her own consent, he lay with her carnally. His skin was cold, and he was the colour of black with a huge hat on his head, his feet were cloven like a beast. All this she observed. At her next meeting, there was twenty or thirty others. On a moonlit night, they all danced until the Devil turned up on a pony, whereupon they all danced crying out, "my Prince, my Prince!" around a fire until the small hours of the morning.

Lillias identified Elspeth Williamson as another of the Devil's Witches at the meeting in her confession, "she is as guilty as I am, my guilt is as sure as God is in Heaven." Then she named another called Agness Currie who supposedly bewitched a child that died... twenty-four years ago!

By August 19th, Lillias, now exhausted by torture inside Dunfermline jail, confessed that she had met the Devil "some hundred times, he came to her house like a shadow, and left like a shadow."[25] This was all witnessed in an audience with the minister, Mr Allan Logan, and his baillies, George Pringle and John Patterson. Alas, these would be Lillias' last words. Before nightfall, she would be found dead from all the exertions put to her from her torture in the jail.

---

25. Her house was at the Ness in the west end of the village and seems to have been a cottage of some notoriety and later used as a Howff for Witches. The windows would look towards the dank braes of the Torry and Golet.

Now came the parish's dilemma: they couldn't give her a Christian burial as Lillias was a confessed but not convicted Witch! Therefore, she may or may not be a Witch. They couldn't burn her as she was confessed, but not convicted... what to do? Well, they decided to bury her in the beach sands between Torryburn and Torres. Just at the high tide mark, and there her bones lay, for the next hundred years anyway!

A Dunfermline painter who would become a favourite of Queen Victoria, (Sir) Joseph Noel Paton, dug up Lillias Adie's bones and took an interest in the story, drawing a sketch of her supposed baptism into the Devil's service from the details of her confession. With his paintings, he had Lillias Adie's bones (skull) in a display as his "collection of curiosities". Sir Joseph Noel Paton would die in 1874, bequeathing his collection to the Hunterian Museum in Glasgow.

Her skull is next mentioned in 1930 (in Black's *Calendar of Cases of Witchcraft*) as being examined by a Doctor from University of St Andrews called Dr William Dow. He describes the skull as from "a small head, with a remarkably receding forehead, from someone with an obvious diseased brain!"

From here, the skull of Lillias Adie is placed in the museum for a while and then vanishes! This author chased the skull from the Hunterian Museum in Glasgow through to the collection of Sir Joseph Noel Paton at the Pittencrieff Museum in Dunfermline and the St Andrews museum where it was last recorded as being on show. It still could be in the Archives of St Andrews, and I'm getting permission

> 731 Lot of Old Keys, &c.
> 732 Lot of Brass Book and Drawer Mountings
> 733 Skull, with other Bones, and portion of the Coffin of Lilias Adie, who, on her own confession, was condemned to be burnt for witchcraft at Torrieburn, but died under torture in the bell-tower of the church, while preparations were in progress for her execution. She was buried within the seamark near Torrieburn, where these relics were obtained on the opening of her grave about 35 years ago
> 734 Skull of Jenny Nettle, celebrated in Scottish Song
> 735 A Number of Plaster Casts of Heads of Noted Individuals

Above the remains of Lillias auctioned off by Mr T Chapman in 1874... bought by Dr William Dow.

to look, which is quite exciting. My own feeling is that, from Dr Dow's examination and comments in 1930, it may be that Lillias suffered from Down's Syndrome. This would be the reason why she was singled out as different and why she was so vulnerable and died so quickly in jail.

My previous book, *Largo's Untold Stories*, has two facial reproductions in it: one, a Pictish woman, the other, an Arctic Explorer who was cannibalised. In the meantime, while I hunt the skull, I approached the Scottish portrait painter Karen Strang to construct a painting of Lillias from her two skull photos.

On the hunt for Lillias Adie's skull, I had a humorous moment with an elderly member of the staff of the Hunterian Museum. The phone conversation follows...

> Me... "Hello, I'm an Author doing some research for a future publication. I'm looking for something that featured in your archive many years ago?"

> Hunterian Museum... "Oooh, yes!"
> Me... "Yes I'm looking for the Skull of a woman, a woman called Lillias Adie."
> Hunterian Museum... "Oooh no, no, she doesn't work here!"
> Me ... "Ha, ha!... no she died a long time ago, she was from Torryburn and—" (A woman buts in the conversation.)
> Hunterian Museum... "Well, she didn't work here. If she died there would have been a collection taken, and I would have dealt with that... No she didn't work here."
> Me... "Ahahaha, I'm sorry you're getting this all wrong, she was a Witch from Torryburn and—" (The woman buts in again.)
> Hunterian Museum... "What did you just call me?"
> Me... "I'm sorry you're getting this all wrong and..."
> Hunterian Museum... "You're a very rude man."... click... brrrrrrrr
> (She hangs up!)

In July 1704, Elizabeth Williamson was arrested in Torryburn and remained in jail till September, apprehended on charges of Witchcraft after Lillias' confession. Following her were Mary Wilson, Janet Whyte, and Jean Bizet on the same charges. Nothing is recorded anywhere of their fate, but with the zeal and hatred of the minister Mr Logan towards Witches, I think they may have burned. His hatred of Witches and his repeated sermons began to wear on his parishioners. In 1709, it's recorded one of his flock spoke out that "Mr Logan was daft when he spoke against the Witches." Margaret Humble was brought forward and forced to repent her claim in the parish court!

In 2014, a rectangular stone was found in the Torryburn beach area. Speculation was that it once was a coffin lid for poor Lillias Addie's remains on the beach. It's a fair size and weight, but my thoughts are that a supposed Witch would not have such expense put to her funeral. A Witch in the community was loathed and hated, and any kindness shown to her from inside the parish that has set out intentions to kill her would be looked at with suspicion. Mary Queen of Scots' Witchcraft Bill of 1563 still carried weight in the law courts and parishes…

> no person seek ony help response or consultation at anysuch users and abusars forasaid of Witchcraft sorcery or Necromancy under pain of deid

Therefore, any such attempt to construct an expensive tomb for her on the beach would bring contempt from the villagers and the church. The stone can be viewed at low tide today, but I'm pretty sure it had another purpose, maybe to do with the famous sea coal mine that once existed here.

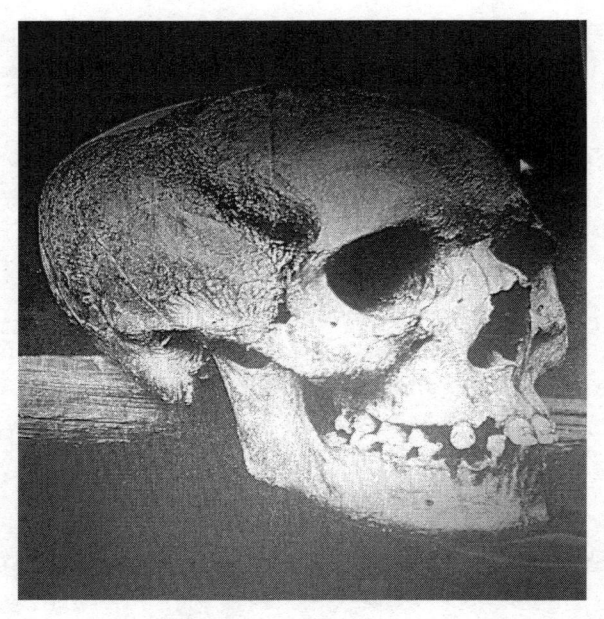

The Skull of Lillias Addie, as photographed in 1874... skull now missing! Painting from the skull photos. Notice the terrible buck teeth.

Sources

GF Black, *A calendar of cases of witchcraft in Scotland* (1938)

J. E. Simpkins, *County Folk-lore: Fife. Vol 7* (1914)

James Wilkie, *Bygone Fife, from Culross to St. Andrews. Traditions, Legends, Folklore and Local History of "the Kingdom"* (1931)

David Webster, *A collection of Rare and Curious Tracts on Witchcraft* (1820)

S. Mc Donald, *The Witches of Fife*

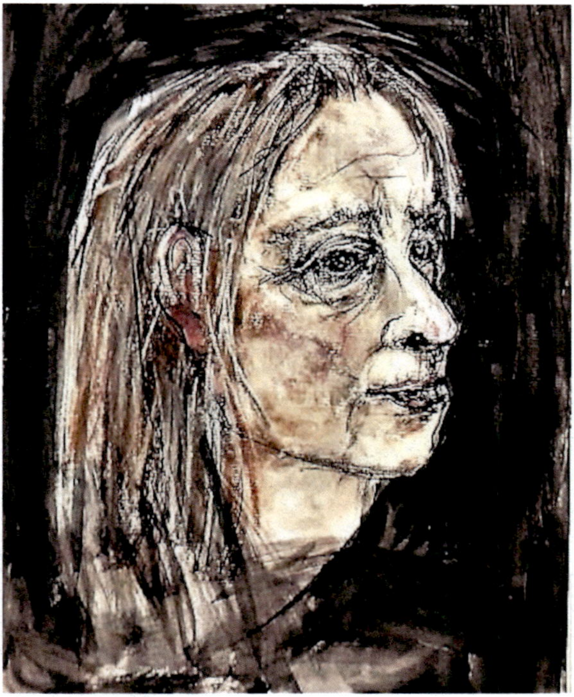

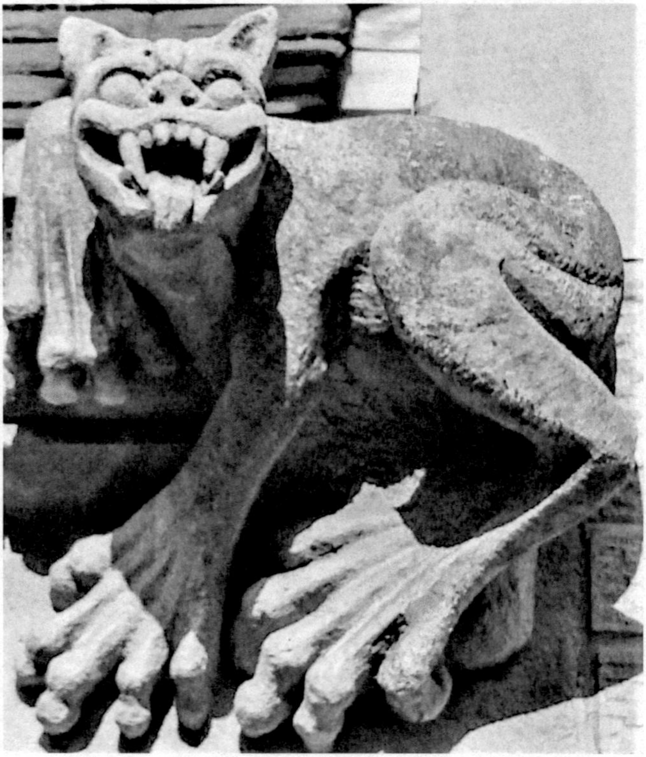

CHAPTER 30

THE CASE OF THE THURSO 'TRANSMOGGYFIER'

In 1232, the Pope Gregory IX declared, "cats were evil and to be associated with the Devil and Witchcraft." Here is where the association of Witches and cats takes its form and leads into the myth of the pointy nosed ugly hag with broom and cat. Every children's story in fables has its quintessential stereotype Witch. The result of Pope Gregory's words was a cat massacre!

We now go on a feline adventure in the Highlands of Scotland and meet the minister there, Mr John Monroe. He was the minister of Halkirk church, where in February of the year 1719, a strange and mysterious Witch hunt started!

William Montgomerie was a stone mason in the small village of Scrabster, which is just over a mile from Thurso. In 1719, the main business of the town was fishing and linen. As a mason, he wasn't short of raw materials, with near four hundred-foot-high rock cliffs surrounding the area. He was now interrogated by the court of Thurso on a complaint that he had been bewitched by cats!

A Barony had been invested on Thurso in the reign of Charles I in 1633, on the Master of Berridale, which was the seat of the Sheriff of Caithness. The courts in use here had baillies who sat on the board as they listened to this strangest of tales.

William Montgomerie was away from home, working on his latest project in Thurso, when a disturbing letter arrived in haste from his wife. She required his immediate return home as a supernatural event was occurring in his own homestead. Up to eight cats had materialised inside his house and were unknown to others in the neighbourhood. The noise they made was incredible, and before long the servants were leaving the service of the house scared out their wits because the cats were speaking in human voices.

William arrived home on the 28th November to find the hairy beasts taking great liberty off the warmth of his fireside. He immediately flew into a rage and attacked them with a dirk and sword. The cats flew everywhere as the violence erupted in the room, but he managed to trap one in a deep wooden chest. The chest had a hole in which the cat had scarpered into, and when the beast stuck its head back out, the sword came down and struck the thing senseless. A servant called Geddes lifted the lid, whereupon the cat was also stabbed in the hindquarters, pinning it to the woodwork with a dirk! It immediately came to life again and broke free; it was then trapped in the room and finally battered to death, then picked up and thrown outside as dead.

By morning, the cat's body had gone! Vanished. Five nights later, the cats returned. When Montgomerie grabbed one and dirked it and battered its head till he knew it was dead... again it was thrown outside... again by morning it had disappeared. He had noticed when stabbing the beast, he drew no blood! It was now entertained that this was an act of Witchcraft; a Witch must be in the neighbourhood and must be found!

The sheriff was called and an inquisition started. By February, a woman living in Owst, just a mile from the

Montgomerie home, was found. While at her own household door, she had collapsed, and her leg had broken and fallen off from the knee. Margaret Nin-Gilbert was elderly and already had a bad fame for Witchcraft. She was arrested and brought before the Magistrates of Thurso on the 8th of February.

Margaret confessed in front of two ministers, a baillie, and four other merchants of Thurso, that she was in compact with the Devil who had appeared to her as a great black horse, sometimes as a black cloud, and then as a Black Hen. She admitted being at Montgomerie's house with other Witches transformed as cats! The Devil himself did conceal them! She claimed two of her friends had died from the blows they took in the house under the assault from Montgomerie, and she herself had been pinned by a dirk in the leg, which she had now lost. It had mortified and broken off. The limb was brought into the courthouse and noted to be, "black and very putrefied".

The other women were named as Margaret Olsone, Jannet Pyper, Helen Andrew, Margaret Callum, and a woman named only as McHuistan from the area of Skaill. Particular attention was given to Margaret Olsone; she was pricked and tortured, revealing several of the Devil's marks upon her while in view of the ministers. Helen Andrew had been so wounded by the assault from Montgomerie in his house, she was so crushed and bruised that she died. McHuistan managed to escape the jail before torture was applied to her and cast herself from the high cliffs of Borrowstoun into the sea and was never seen again.

The Lord Advocate Dundas some weeks later heard of

the case and sent letters demanding fault with the proper proceedings of the trial. A commission from the central authorities was the usual practice, but it had not been adhered to. The baillies admitted faults and apologised on the grounds they had communicated with the Earl of Breadalbane[26] alone. The case was then dropped, and the accused Witches were released... but it was too late for Margaret Nin-Gilbert, she had died from her injuries and the complications of her leg in the prison in Thurso.

SOURCES

GF Black, *A calendar of cases of witchcraft in Scotland* (1938)

Robert Chambers, *Domestic Annals of Scotland* vol. III (1859–61)

Charles Kirkpatrick Sharpe, *A historical account of the belief in Witchcraft in Scotland* (1884)

---

26. John Campbell, 2nd Earl of Breadalbane from 1717.

An English gentleman called Edmund Burt was stationed in Sutherland in the late 1720s. He wrote letters to a friend in London describing his accommodation and the natives and customs in the Northwestern Highlands for a period of over ten years. It is a rare view that gives insight into the lives of the people who toiled the land. The information is a window into the beliefs and struggles of a crofting race of people who would be forcefully migrated in the following years with the disturbances of rebellion and Highland clearance. But he also documented the burning of the last Witch in Scotland in 1727, in Dornoch, where we have already visited in this book. There would be nine more years till the final absolution on the Witch hunts. I finish my book with his thoughts, which are very relevant...

> I am almost ashamed to ask seriously how it comes to pass that in populous cities, among the most wicked and abandoned wretches, this art of Witchcraft should not be discovered; and yet that so many little villages and obscure places should be nurseries for Witchcraft? But the thing is not worth speaking of, any further than that it is greatly to be wished that any such law should be annulled, which subjects the lives of human creatures to the weakness of an ignorant magistrate or jury, for the crime of which they never had the power to be guilty. This might free them from the miseries and insults these poor wretches suffer when unhappily fallen under the imputation in this country of Sutherland.
>
> Edmund Burt... Sutherland 1727

NAMES OF THE KNOWN FIFE ACCUSED WITCHES FROM KIRKCALDY TO CRAIL

Naturally, coming from Largo, my heart lies in the coastal Fife Witch cases, and from the heights of the near 1,000-foot-high Largo Law, I can see the coastline from Kirkcaldy to Crail. With this I must dedicate this latest book from me to the east coast Witches—from Kirkcaldy to Crail—the ones known are as follows…

1. Margaret Reid ………………………………… no date ……… Kirkcaldy
2. Katherine Shaw ………………………………… no date ……… Kirkcaldy
3. Margaret Williamsone ……………………… 11/8/1597 ……… Kirkcaldy
4. Janet Bennetie ………………………………… 17/8/1597 ……… Kirkcaldy
5. Beigis Blakatt ………………………………… 17/8/1597 ……… Kirkcaldy
6. Margaret Elder ………………………………… 17/8/1597 ……… Kirkcaldy
7. Goillis Hoggone ……………………………… 17/8/1597 ……… Kirkcaldy
8. Margaret Hoicon ……………………………… 17/8/1597 ……… Kirkcaldy
9. Isabel Jak ………………………………………… 17/8/1597 ……… Kirkcaldy
10. Thomas Jamieson …………………………… 17/8/1597 ……… Kirkcaldy
11. Isobell Jonstoun ……………………………… 17/8/1597 ……… Kirkcaldy
12. Bessie Osatt …………………………………… 17/8/1597 ……… Kirkcaldy
13. William Patersone …………………………… 17/8/1597 ……… Kirkcaldy
14. Marion Rutherford …………………………… 17/8/1597 ……… Kirkcaldy
15. Bessie Scott …………………………………… 17/8/1597 ……… Kirkcaldy
16. Dorathie Oliphant …………………………… 16/6/1604 ……… Kirkcaldy
17. Agness Anstruther …………………………………… 1614 ……… Kirkcaldy
18. Issobel Johnestwone ………………………………… 1614 ……… Kirkcaldy
19. Marioun Rutherford ………………………… 13/5/1621 ……… Kirkcaldy

20.	Helen Birrell	4/4/1626	Kirkcaldy
21.	Janet Pirie	4/4/1626	Kirkcaldy
22.	Janet Stark	4/4/1626	Kirkcaldy
23.	William Coke	12/1633	Kirkcaldy
24.	Alison Dick	12/1633	Kirkcaldy
25.	Margaret Bannatyne	19/7/1638	Kirkcaldy
26.	Christian Wilson	19/7/1638	Kirkcaldy
27.	Margaret Douglas	23/5/1639	Kirkcaldy
28.	Margaret Lindsay	10/9/1640	Kirkcaldy
29.	Isobel Thomson	28/4/1647	Kirkcaldy
30.	Janet…?	5/5/1626	Dysart
31.	Elspett Neilsoun	9/1626	Dysart
32.	Annas Munk	21/9/1626	Dysart
33.	Helen Wilsoun	21/11/1626	Dysart
34.	Eupham Dauling	27/9/1627	Dysart
35.	Katherine Crystie	17/11/1627	Dysart
36.	Helen Bissat	11/3/1630	Dysart
37.	William Broun	11/3/1630	Dysart
38.	Janet Galbraith	11/3/1630	Dysart
39.	Bessie Guiddale	11/3/1630	Dysart
40.	Janet Scot	11/3/1630	Dysart
41.	Katherine Chrystie	16/3/1630	Dysart
42.	Janet Beverage	21/4/1630	Dysart
43.	Margaret Dasoun	21/4/1630	Dysart
44.	Alison Neving	21/4/1630	Dysart

45.	Elspet Watsoun	8/7/1630	Dysart
46.	John Patowne	6/4/1637	Dysart
47.	Marioun Grig	12/7/1638	Dysart
48.	Margaret Wilson	10/8/1642	Dysart
49.	Lillias Baxter	7/2/1644	Dysart
50.	Janet Rankine	7/2/1644	Dysart
51.	Margaret Cunningham	27/3/1644	Dysart
52.	Agnes Bennettie	27/3/1644	Dysart
53.	Margaret Halkhead	27/3/1644	Dysart
54.	Margaret Young	2/10/1644	Dysart
55.	Elizabeth Simpsone	6/11/1649	Dysart
56.	Margaret Beverage	1658	Dysart
57.	John Corse	2/2/1658	Dysart
58.	Issobell Mawyer	16/3/1626	Wemyss
59.	Helen Darumpill	13/4/1626	Wemyss
60.	Patrik Landrok	13/4/1626	Wemyss
61.	Jonnet Pedie	13/4/1626	Wemyss
62.	Elizabeth Ross	6/6/1626	Wemyss
63.	Jonnet Dampstar	20/6/1626	Wemyss
64.	Janet Wilkie	20/3/1630	Wemyss
65.	Janet Durie	27/12/1638	Wemyss
66.	Janet Small	20/10/1603	Largo
67.	Beatrix Trallis	22/12/1603	Largo
68.	Christen Trallis	22/12/1603	Largo
69.	Jonet Wylie	6/8/1644	Largo
70.	Thomas Wilson	1653	Largo

71.	Grizzle	1500s	St Monans
72.	Tibbie Dowie	1549	St Monans
73.	Maggie Morgan	1651	St Monans
74.	Elspeth Morrison	6/4/1676	St Monans
75.	Janet Loquhour	15/3/1593	Pittenweem
76.	Jonett Foggow	9/6/1597	Pittenweem
77.	Beatrix Forgesoun	9/6/1597	Pittenweem
78.	Jonet Willeaamsoun	9/6/1597	Pittenweem
79.	Fritte Gutter	6/10/1597	Pittenweem
80.	Isabel Flic	20/7/1600	Pittenweem
81.	Wife of John Dawson	3/11/1643	Pittenweem
82.	Margaret Kingow	13/12/1643	Pittenweem
83.	Margaret Horsburgh	18/12/1643	Pittenweem
84.	Wife of John Crombie	21/12/1643	Pittenweem
85.	Wife of Thomas Wanderson	21/1/1644	Pittenweem
86.	Beaty Dote, of St Monans	3/7/1644	Pittenweem
87.	Christian Dote, of St Monans	3/7/1644	Pittenweem
88.	Christian Roch	7/11/1644	Pittenweem
89.	Margaret Myrton	1/6/1644	Pittenweem
90.	Margaret Balfour	1/6/1644	Pittenweem
91.	Janet Cornfoot	1/6/1704	Pittenweem
92.	Isobel Adam	1704	Pittenweem
93.	Mrs White	1/6/1704	Pittenweem
94.	Margaret Jack	13/6/1704	Pittenweem
95.	Margaret Wallace	13/6/1704	Pittenweem
96.	Janet Horseburgh	14/6/1704	Pittenweem

97.	Lillias Wallace	14/6/1704	Pittenweem
98.	Thomas Brown	14/6/1704	Pittenweem
99.	Nicholas Lawson	14/6/1704	Pittenweem
100.	Eppie Laing	8/1643	Anstruther
101.	Isobell Dairsie	24/1/1644	Anstruther
102.	Elizabeth Dick	4/1701	Anstruther E.
103.	Euphame Locoir	1590	Crail
104.	Geillis Gray	22/2/1599	Crail
105.	Margaret Wod	30/1/1621	Crail
106.	Marjorie Pattersone	30/1/1621	Crail
107.	Agnes Wallace	30/10/1643	Crail
108.	Grillies Robertson	1673	Crail

AFTERWORD

It's fitting that today 24th May 2022, while my publisher has just fought his way through editing the second part of this book and sent it to me to correct and read through again... the news breaks that the Church of Scotland has...

> acknowledged and expressed regret over the wrongs done to those accused of Witchcraft. The Reverend Professor Susan Hardman bought the motion forward today and it was accepted by the General Assembly of the Church of Scotland.

The repeal of the Witchcraft Act in 1736 brought howls of protest from Ministers, this following letter gives the feeling amongst the Witch-hating Ministers...

> May 25th 1758 the Reverent Mr Wesley (Sunderland Parish) his journal page for the day:
> It is true likewise that the English in general and indeed most of men of learning in Europe have given up all accounts of Witches and apperations as mere old wifes tales! I am sorry for it! I willingly take this opportunity of offering my solem protest against it. Giving up belief in Witchcraft is in effect giving up the Bible.

The Scottish Government just a few weeks back issued the same apology. But the process started nearly 20 years back in Scotland. In 2002 in East Lothian, Mr Dr Gordon Froome, the current incumbent of the hereditary Baronial court of Prestongrange and Dolphinstoun, exorcised his legal authority to pardon the 81 Witches executed in the area 1590–1679. Shortly after the Baron courts were stripped of power. By this act the Berwick Witches were pardoned.

My own feelings on this wave of sympathy, are it takes 266 years for the Church to acknowledge the murders of those they called Witches, committed in the name of their God—while preaching love thy neighbour. The latest news on the mass imminent shut down and closure of the Fife churches must seem the end days for Religion. Perhaps they should have practiced what they preached?

I'm currently about to be a grandfather this year. (Hello Alfie!) With this I am constructing a family tree through the Mason line of my family (mothers maiden name and my middle) In the process two Witches have been identified... one burnt in St Andrews in 1644, the other never made it alive out of the dungeon in 1597.

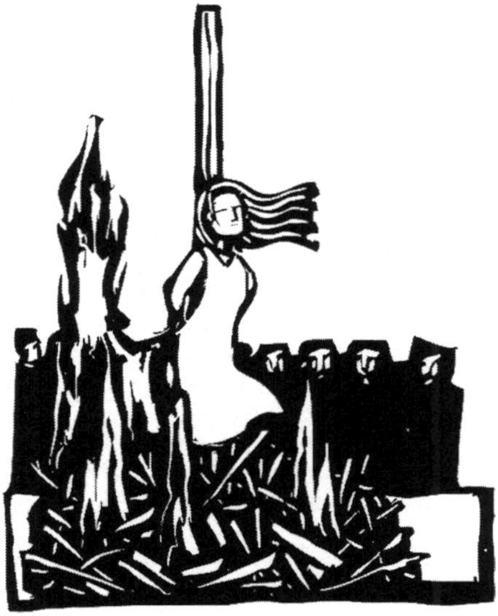

More HISTORY from Guardbridge Books.

Scotland's Untold Stories
also by Leonard Low

Fascinating stories from throughout Scottish history—forgotten stories and overlooked details about well-known figures. Leonard Low explores the dark and mysterious, the tragic and the heroic, and brings the stories to life with his evocative writing.

"Leonard Low brings dead history alive." —Dundee Courier

A Horrid Deed: The Life and Death of Joe the Quilter
by Robert N. Smith

A gentle old man, murdered in his modest cottage in 1826. The case was a sensation, but never solved. Part true crime, part social history, this book reveals the lives—and deaths—of the common people usually overlooked.

"In Robert Smith's capable hands, readers will find themselves enthralled in a mystery for the ages while steeping themselves in a fascinating time and place too often forgotten."

—James Wolfinger, Prof. History, Illinois State U.

All are available at our website and online retailers.

http://guardbridgebooks.co.uk